WISDOM IN HINDSIGHT

A Practical Playbook for Better Decisions, Better Habits, and Better Outcomes.

ROBERT H. DARROW

This book is not intended for use as a source of legal, business, accounting, or financial advice. Readers are encouraged to seek the services of competent professionals in these fields for expert advice.

Any opinion expressed in this book is that of Robert Darrow and not necessarily that of Darrow Bentley, LLC DBA Strive Retirement Group, an independent advisory firm.

Many names of the individuals in this book have been changed; however, the general storyline remains intact. Any perceived slights of specific people or organizations are unintentional.

Certified Financial Planner Board of Standards Center for Financial Planning, Inc. owns and licenses the certification marks CFP® and CERTIFIED FINANCIAL PLANNER™ in the United Stated to Certified Financial Planner Board of Standards, Inc., which authorizes individuals who successfully complete the organization's initial and ongoing certification requirements to use the certification marks.

Published by Robert Darrow
Longwood, Florida

ISBN: 979-8-9955359-0-4 (paperback)
ISBN: 979-8-9955359-1-1 (ebook)

First Edition

Cover and interior formatting by KUHN Design Group | kuhndesigngroup.com

Printed in the United States of America

To April, my biggest supporter.

To my friends who encouraged me to put pen to paper.

To the mentors and leaders that have
inspired me throughout my career.

CONTENTS

INTRODUCTION

*"It's not your starting pay that matters;
it's your ending pay."*

The eleven words, spoken casually by my father one evening at the dinner table, shaped one of my earliest career decisions and, in hindsight, probably more than I realized at the time.

I was deciding between two entry-level job offers. The first paid $9.50 an hour, working in accounts payable for a copier company that would later go bankrupt. The second paid $9.00 an hour at a small but growing payroll processor. Logic suggested I should take the higher-paying job. Instead, I chose the payroll company and stayed there for twenty-six years.

That's the thing about wisdom: You rarely recognize its value in the moment. What feels like an ordinary conversation can quietly influence decisions for decades.

I didn't attend the school of hard knocks, but I also wasn't born with a silver spoon in my mouth. I didn't listen as well as I should have in my more formative years, and "self-motivated" would have been a generous description of my younger self.

In high school, while working part-time in the sporting goods department of a local store, my manager once offered some memorable feedback. As I stood there placing individual price stickers on a case of tennis balls, he told me I had a rare talent: the ability to look busy while accomplishing absolutely nothing.

It's quite possible that I look at things a little differently than most people.

Just the other day, after taking the garbage out to the curb, I heard a loud screeching sound. By the time I arrived at the scene, it was clear that my trash can had been involved in a hit-and-run incident. I wasn't particularly emotionally attached to the can, even though it had been with me for many years, so I knew it was time to say goodbye. There wasn't much visible damage, but it was certainly inoperable.

My wife and I stood there for a few minutes before bursting into laughter, trying to figure out how you throw out something whose sole purpose is to throw out things. Spoiler alert: You put a sign on it that says, TAKE ME, PLEASE!

Most of us have daily moments that seem insignificant at the time, until they quietly turn into stories we tell later. And depending on the patience of the friends and loved ones I surround myself with, those stories often turn into unsolicited life lessons.

The broken garbage can raised several questions for me. Why is it so hard to let go of things that no longer serve us? Why do we cling to outdated habits, inefficient processes, or beliefs that quietly steer our lives off course? And perhaps most importantly, how do we course-correct, positioning ourselves for better outcomes? If only we could put a TAKE ME, PLEASE! sign on our own mental clutter.

Having spent most of my career in and around the financial services industry, I've noticed that at some point it feels almost like a rite of passage to write a book. Unfortunately, many of those efforts read more like extended marketing brochures than genuine works of reflection. Business development is not my goal here, though you'll see some of my experience as a CERTIFIED FINANCIAL PLAN-NER™ woven naturally into a number of these stories. And just to be safe, you'll also find a legal disclosure tucked somewhere near the inside cover of the book.

Getting back to stories, my wife regularly reminds me that I need new ones. I usually joke that it would be much easier to simply find new people to whom I can tell the same stories.

But on a more serious note, a good friend I first met in the late 1990s, when I hired him as a rookie sales representative, recently reminded me of a story I told him twenty-seven years ago while driving to his first sales meeting. At the time, I used stories as a wrapper for certain training ideas I was trying to convey. What surprised me wasn't that I remembered the story; it was that he did. It genuinely caught me off guard that something said so long ago had resonated for decades.

I can't claim that my stories always land perfectly. Hopefully, hiring a professional editor for this book will help keep me on track. I've also tested many of these anecdotes with friends and colleagues who know they're expected to give candid, unfiltered feedback.

I've learned, however, that stories tend to go sideways when they involve body parts, illness, or injury.

I quickly "unretired" after a short flirtation with rest and relaxation in 2021, when I realized I wasn't quite ready to hear weekly updates from the senior golfing group about their prostates. They probably have no idea how influential they were in my decision to go back to work.

On Monday nights after our tennis league matches, we meet in the clubhouse for beer and pizza. One week I launched into a far too detailed, play-by-play account of an orthopedic appointment for a herniated disc. One league partner—we'll call him Mitch—politely excused himself from the table. I assumed he was heading to the restroom, but I was soon surprised when a tablemate picked up his phone. Mitch was on the line, asking if anyone wanted to join him at a different bar up the road since he had already secured a table.

Laughter followed as my friend switched to speakerphone. Mitch explained that he'd heard about my back issues before. They weren't interesting the first time, and he didn't see the story improving with a second telling.

Rather than finding an entirely new group of friends to endure the same stories, I decided to put my thoughts on paper. What began as a weekly email to a handful of referral partners gradually became a series of essays. As that collection grew, I noticed recurring themes that eventually began to resemble chapters. With a bit of focus, and some unearned confidence, I suddenly had something that looked like a book.

I hope you don't take this book too seriously. I've never taken myself very seriously. And between artificial intelligence and vanity presses, getting published these days isn't particularly difficult.

Justifying my journalism degree over the past thirty-five years, however, has been more challenging given that I went straight into the business world and never worked in media. Consider this box partially checked.

As I write this in my home office, behind me are floor-to-ceiling bookshelves filled with titles on self-help, leadership, finance, sales, and other nonfiction topics. My special skill is reading somewhere between half and two-thirds of each book, never quite finishing. The reason? Many of them would have been better served as a long essay, journal, or booklet rather than a full-length book.

My goal with this narrative blend of observation, advice, and attempted humor is simple: to keep you engaged from beginning to end. If I succeed, and you find it worthwhile, I hope you'll recommend the book to someone else.

And before we dive in, I should say this: The stories that follow aren't meant to impress, instruct, or persuade in any heavy-handed way. I've also changed some names and altered the events slightly in some situations so as not to embarrass anyone. They're simply moments, small, ordinary experiences that revealed something useful only after enough time had passed. Which brings us, appropriately, to expiration dates.

NO EXPIRATION DATE FOR GOOD ADVICE

Every few months my wife and I organize the pantry, donate things we didn't end up using, and, in her case, reluctantly throw out items that are past their expiration date. This guarantees a nonproductive debate, as we both have completely different views of what these dates actually indicate. In my case, all three variations—"best by," "expire," and "use by"—mean immediately after that date passes, you don't eat or drink the product in question. She feels that those dates are merely suggestions, ones she very rarely adheres to. We have paused more than one heated discussion with a Google search comparing what the terms mean.

Imagine if advice came with a suggested time frame for optimal freshness, something we could all check before blindly applying it years later. Unfortunately, it doesn't, so we must determine on our own when the advice, which may have been good at one point, is no longer valid. The best advice, however, withstands the test of time, not requiring an expiration date, but maybe just some slight tweaks around the edges to make the topic more modern.

Gone are the days when I could drive home a point by comparing high-definition televisions with their predecessors, the picture tube TVs. The current generation doesn't know what a picture tube is, so any metaphors that incorporate it are pointless. However, a lesson can still be conveyed by simply updating the analogy to comparing the now inefficient Google search to a quick verbal interaction with your desktop digital assistant. I think the current generation may be surprised to know that we used to be excited when our parents let us have a nineteen-inch black and white TV in our bedroom. They may be even more shocked when we explain how to strategically open and read a folding map while driving down the highway, our early version of GPS.

As would be expected, some of the best advice I have received over my lifetime came from my parents. And as the title of this book would suggest, I only realized the value of this wisdom in hindsight. Although I have spent almost my entire career in sales and sales leadership, notably in the financial services sector, I'm not a particularly gregarious person. After being volunteered to take a sales personality test so our company could screen a potential new vendor, the feedback given to our executive team at the time was that "Bob likes to get invited to the party—he just doesn't want to go." Upon hearing this assessment and understanding how accurate it was, they signed a five-figure contract.

I entered sales leadership when I realized I was much more comfortable watching awards ceremonies from my seat. It was far more desirable standing on the side of the stage taking pictures of my team "high-fiving" the sales VP versus personally walking to the podium to give a top performer speech.

Although sales and sales leadership would end up becoming a large part of my career progression, it was at a much younger age when I began to develop the skills necessary to succeed.

Since my parents always referred to my job as a "career in marketing" (I've never held one position in the marketing department), my mother would be surprised to know she launched my sales career at the ripe old age of ten.

How so?

Although my first sales job was likely in elementary school when I would buy a pack of Bubble Yum for twenty-five cents and divide up the five pieces, selling them to my classmates for a dime each, the job most kids wanted was the neighborhood paper route.

It may be hard to believe, but it wasn't too long ago that you had to wait until the following morning to get your "news" for the day.

Although it depended on how efficient your delivery person was, the newspaper typically arrived around 7:00 a.m. Putting child labor laws aside, your delivery person was usually a kid on a bike, typically with questionable aim. Your hope was they could land the rolled-up paper within a few yards of your doorstep so the neighbors could be spared the view of you in your bathrobe, or maybe even worse.

Growing up in Connecticut, our newspaper was actually an afternoon publication, making it the ideal after-school job. I'm hopeful the young man that delivered *The News-Times* in our neighborhood ended up being a tremendous success, but let's just say his career didn't get off to a great start. The paper often arrived late, if it even was delivered at all. So, when I was ten years old, my parents encouraged me to approach him and offer to "buy" the route from him. He soundly rejected the idea. I wondered out loud, why would someone who obviously wasn't good at, or interested in, the job prevent someone else from getting it? I had a lot to learn!

I really wanted this job because the pay was lucrative. You would get five cents for each paper you delivered, and if you were really good, the holiday bonuses could be very generous as well. Around this same time, our town was opening a recycling center, one of the first of its kind. With help from my mother, I decided to pivot from delivering the papers each day to picking them up for recycling each week. I would carry a ruler with me while pulling my Radio Flyer wagon house-to-house.

My fee was one penny per inch of newspaper, payable on the spot. Oh, and feel free to round up if you don't have the right coin. It turned out the pay was even better, I could work on my own schedule, and it was just one day a week versus seven! However, I would never have come up with this idea because I was too emotionally attached to my desire to "rescue" the community from their awful delivery experience. It turned out what I really needed—something most of us do at some point—was someone without emotional attachment to look at the situation from a completely different angle.

That early lesson—that perspective matters as much as effort—stuck with me long after the wagon, ruler, and recycling runs were gone.

Once sales became a full-time profession as an adult, and knowing that my parents still told their friends I was in marketing, I wasn't surprised when others shied away from the title of sales representative.

Far too often, I would see salespeople refer to themselves as "consultants." Some companies aren't very strict about what title their business development reps put in email signatures or LinkedIn profiles. Others, however, veer into the inflated, if not outright misleading. Senior Vice President of Solutions Architecture and Client Outcomes, anyone?

Whenever I hired salespeople, it was a firm rule that their title was exactly that: sales representative. Why not sales consultant? That doesn't seem like much of a stretch, does it? It is.

The distinction between consulting and sales lies in allegiance. A consultant's obligation is to the client, even when that means recommending a competing solution. A salesperson's obligation, however ethical, remains to their product. If sales reps working for a single company were truly consulting, they would inevitably have to recommend a competitor, at least occasionally. That would be a quick path to unemployment.

So why are salespeople so eager to change their titles, and what does that say about society's perception of the profession?

Most of us grew up steeped in the negative connotations of sales. The door-to-door vacuum cleaner demo began with someone dumping dirt on your carpet. The dinner was interrupted by an unwelcome telemarketing call. Used car lots, timeshares, mall kiosks, boiler rooms, the list goes on. Over time, sales came to mean pressure, concealment, and manipulation, not advice, transparency, or trust. Those early experiences quietly trained us to brace ourselves whenever someone said, "Can I show you something?"

The first time I truly understood how critical the sales department is to an organization came during my summer breaks helping open pizza delivery restaurants. Domino's dominated the industry at the time, but I worked for a small local chain that had developed something close to a cult following in parts of Connecticut. About three weeks before opening our fourth location, I told one of the owners I thought we were woefully unprepared. We still needed uniforms, menus, flyers, trash collection, signage, probably even more than I can remember.

I suggested we grab the phone book (yes, this was pre-internet) and start calling vendors. He had a much simpler solution. He left for a couple of hours and came back with a banner that read: PIZZA PLACE COMING SOON.

You can't call your boss crazy and keep your job, but I was curious how this would solve our crisis. "Let the product sales reps come to us," he said. "Much easier." And sure enough, that banner above the door triggered a flood of vendors offering quotes. Within days, we had multiple options for each service and opened on schedule.

We didn't need consultants. We just needed sales representatives, and enough conviction to evaluate product, price, and service commitments.

I wasn't passionate enough about food to build a career in restaurant management, but I carried that lesson forward. Those sales reps saved us. They helped us open on time so we could generate revenue immediately. Wherever I went after that, and whatever role I held, I wore the title of *sales representative* as a badge of honor, not something to disguise or apologize for.

No doubt some people reading this hold titles that include words like *marketing, business development, consultant,* or *account manager.* I would encourage you to switch back to *sales representative* and see what changes.

You might be surprised how much power there is, professionally and personally, in simply owning what you do.

CHAPTER 2

FROM THE DELI COUNTER TO THE CHECKOUT LINE

The best sales book I have ever read was one you've never heard of. Okay, well, maybe you worked in payroll or insurance sales in the mid-nineties, but I'll assume that's not too many of you. *Expecting Referrals* by Scott Kramnick was published in 1994 when I was just a couple of years into my sales career. It wasn't widely distributed and has been out of print for quite some time. Scott was a successful insurance agent in the Washington, DC, area, and our company hired him to be the keynote speaker at a few of our regional kickoff meetings. They did so with the hope that he could help our teams increase their effectiveness at soliciting client referrals.

As with any professional development book that's over thirty years old, there are certainly suggestions that are outdated. There really were no electronic ways to communicate or market products back then, so you won't get any ideas on email marketing or social media in this book. And yet this book still stands the test of time.

What got me thinking about this book again after all this time? Recently I needed to send something certified mail, so I stopped into the post office for what I thought would be about a four-dollar transaction. After helping me with this simple task, the postal clerk asked me if I needed a book of stamps. "Well, yes, I do!" I said. Then he replied, probably with very little sales training, "What else?" *Wow! That's the deli method of referral-based selling*, I said to myself.

If you don't know what the deli method is, then go into your local grocery store, head to the deli counter, and ask for a half pound of turkey. They'll fill your order and then ask you, "What else?" Two words, that's it. And then again, and again. Knowing you only came there for turkey, you'll leave the deli counter with turkey, ham, pastrami, and Swiss cheese. Stay strong so it doesn't get even more expensive than that!

How does this apply to B2B sales? When a referral source offers up an introduction to a valuable client, thank them, and then politely ask, "Who else can I help?" Try it, you'll be pleasantly surprised! Don't stop asking until they're done providing you with great leads.

Retail's quiet closers exist everywhere; you just might not know it when you see it.

When we moved into our current home, we decided to install hedges around the entire perimeter. They were visually appealing, provided privacy, and required little ongoing maintenance. The one recurring task was mulch, about eight cubic yards every twelve to eighteen months.

Unlike some of my neighbors, I opted not to spend an entire weekend hauling and spreading bags myself. Instead, I called a commercial mulch company to ask what it would cost for them to bring in one of their massive trucks and use high-powered blowers to handle the job.

Ten yards was the minimum, though I only needed eight. After a little research and some quick math, I concluded that since they were already spraying the mulch, it made sense to buy the ten yards and have the extra two blown into the woods. Efficient enough.

That worked well, until it didn't.

When I called to schedule service, I was told the new minimum was twenty yards. Residential jobs, it turns out, were no longer worth their time. Their oversized rigs didn't fare well under the oak tree canopy lining our streets. Twenty yards made no sense to me. I couldn't justify wasting twelve yards.

No problem, I thought. I'd just order bagged mulch online from a big-box home improvement store and have one or two pallets delivered.

The website proudly advertised free delivery. A pallet, however, consists of somewhere between sixty and eighty two-cubic-foot bags, roughly five yards. Even spreading it myself, this was still more rational than discarding twelve yards of bulk mulch.

Then I saw the delivery fee: $79.

Free delivery, it turned out, applied only to orders of six bags or fewer. Anything beyond that triggered the charge. I opened the chat box to ask how this could make sense. The customer service representative, clearly reading from a well-worn FAQ, suggested that I place ten separate orders of six bags each to qualify for free delivery.

Two problems immediately came to mind.

First, I'm certain ten separate deliveries of mulch would permanently disqualify me from ever claiming concern about my carbon footprint. Second, if my credit card company didn't flag ten identical transactions from the same retailer as suspicious, I'd seriously question their fraud protection systems.

So it was back to the store, a few bags at a time, like the old days.

My pickup truck could generously be described as a "trucklet." With a bed barely four and a half feet long, it makes an old El Camino look like a Ford F-350. If I stack carefully, exceed every recommended height limit, and drive painfully slowly for the three miles home, I can fit exactly twenty-one bags per trip.

I was prepared for three or four trips. And before you suggest that my time was worth more than the $79 delivery fee, understand that by this point I was operating entirely on principle.

After wrestling a heavy utility cart through checkout on my first run, I decided to try a different approach on trip number two. I went to the cashier first, paid for twenty bags in advance, and planned to pull my truck around afterward.

Same quantity. Same brand. Different cashier.

She refused to sell it to me.

"I need you to go to aisle 54," she said, "and load the mulch from there. The name-brand mulch outside is 1.5 cubic feet for $3.98. The generic mulch in aisle 54 is $3.33 for two cubic feet."

My quick, mental, don't-show-your-work math told me this was roughly a 40 percent savings.

I explained that I had already started the project using the name brand and didn't want to mix products around the shrubs.

She looked at me, unimpressed.

"Really?" she said. "Brown mulch is brown mulch. I won't allow you to do it." And so, she won the debate, and I learned a valuable lesson.

What stuck with me wasn't the mulch itself, but how inefficient the process became in the name of efficiency. Minimums, thresholds, delivery rules, and rigid policies all make sense when viewed in bulk. They're logical at scale. But zoom in to the individual level and that logic often breaks down. What's optimized for the system isn't always practical, or even rational, for the person navigating it.

Whether it's home improvement, business decisions, or financial planning, the cleanest solution on paper frequently ignores the real-world variables that matter most.

As young sales representatives with unhealthy levels of drive and competitive spirit, my colleagues and I would grab the stack rankings each Friday to see who brought in the most new accounts for the week. First place was all that mattered—we didn't look too far past that line. We thought we were so clever when we justified our second-place (or worse) finishes with, "I would have been number one if it weren't for the sales prevention department." That's the name we gave the service team whenever they rejected one of our new client cases as incomplete.

As I reflect years later, it's obvious we were just making excuses and would have been better off submitting accurate files in the first place.

So, while offering a belated apology to my operations partners from thirty years ago, I still believe that much like the mulch example, there are times when the folks in corporate cause more problems than solutions.

An example of a simple transaction that should almost go unnoticed during your day is buying lunch. One of the more popular sandwich shops in town went through rapid expansion and became a regional chain. To build a national footprint, they needed capital, and the most logical solution was to partner with a private equity firm to fund their growth. That partnership also gave them access to the vast resources a large firm can provide, including accounting, marketing, human resources, and some version of a business intelligence or analytics department.

Not that I need to rush through lunch, but if I'm not entertaining someone, or being entertained by a referral partner, thirty to forty-five minutes seems about right for this daily break. As I stepped up to the counter, just as a lengthy line began forming behind me, the cashier asked nine separate questions to complete my order.

Don't get me wrong. I appreciate thoroughness. But I couldn't help wondering how many of those questions were unnecessary, already answered, or could have been assumed. I'm certain they would decline my complimentary consulting offer, but a few examples came to mind:

- "What name should I put on the order?" The one printed on the credit card I just handed you.

- "What size drink would you like with your combo?" The one that comes with the combo.

- "For here or to go?" You've wrapped everything the same way since COVID.

The inability to get in and out of my sandwich shop in a timely manner may be a minor disruption to my day, but far more important tasks, like financial planning and crafting an estate plan, carry much more weight. Let me give you an example.

It's difficult to find a definitive study to cite, but it is widely believed that more than half of all revocable trusts remain unfunded or only partially funded. In other words, families do the heavy lifting, meeting with an estate planning attorney, drafting the documents, and paying for the trust, yet the final and most essential step of transferring assets into the trust never gets completed. Many assume the signed documents are the finish line. Most attorneys would tell you they're only the starting point.

There are plenty of published studies on how many Americans have a written financial plan, and those numbers are even more discouraging. Depending on the research, somewhere between 19 and 32 percent of working adults have taken the time to map out their retirement, insurance needs, college funding, major purchases, charitable intentions, and other long-term goals. Failing to take these steps is the financial equivalent of embarking upon a long, unfamiliar road trip and choosing not to use GPS.

At my advisory firm, we recently implemented one of the leading financial planning software platforms as we continue looking for ways to add value to our existing relationships. With both new and existing clients, the process begins with a comprehensive questionnaire covering all aspects of a family's financial life.

How many of our clients or prospects will complete this nine-page interrogation? Given that we primarily work with busy business owners, my guess is fewer than the national averages cited above. So, while working with an existing client recently, and inspired by my newly created "sandwich shop rule," I prefilled the answers I already knew and eliminated the sections that didn't apply. It took less than ten minutes and doing so cut my clients' workload in half. I'll be tracking completion rates moving forward, and I'm confident our results will exceed national norms.

A plan provides clarity, direction, and peace of mind for a family's future. Because, in the end, the problem is rarely that we don't know what to do. It's that somewhere along the way, the process became more complicated than it needed to be.

CHAPTER 3

WHAT WE NOTICE, WHAT WE REMEMBER, WHAT WE BELIEVE

The word *bias* often comes with negative connotations, as well it probably should. But biases are present in everything we do or say, and are very rarely obvious to us when we are looking through tainted lenses.

Whether it's confirmation bias, recency bias, or scarcity effect, many of our decisions and views are influenced by these predispositions.

Each year, every sports team in every league begins the season undefeated—no wins, no losses. There's nothing quite like Opening Day for fans, knowing their team is technically tied for first place (and last, for that matter) in the division.

Of course, it doesn't take long for reality to set in. Absent some phenomenon I'm unaware of, every season will end with a collective .500 record across the league. We know the word *fan* is shorthand for "fanatic," someone with obsessive enthusiasm for a single thing, so expecting calm logic when your favorite baseball team starts 14–14 after the first month is simply too much to ask. Instead, social media warriors take over, insisting the front office be fired and core players traded or released.

Most professional sports leagues in the US have between thirty and thirty-two teams. Unlike fans, league commissioners crave parity, keeping as many teams in contention as long as possible to drive drama and ratings. In the commissioner's perfect world, there would be no dynasties or perennial cellar dwellers. In a thirty-team league, every franchise would win the championship once every thirty years. Of course, that never happens. There will always be the Yankees, Lakers, Patriots, and Montreal Canadiens, but that doesn't stop leagues from introducing rules designed to flatten the competitive curve.

So, just for fun, let's look at the New York Mets. As a lifelong Mets fan, I'm painfully aware the team is known more for disappointment than for the two seasons in which they hoisted the World Series trophy. The Mets began in 1962 as an expansion team, replacing the Dodgers and Giants after they left New York for California. At the end of the 2025 season, the franchise had completed sixty-four years of baseball. If 2026 turns out as promising as it looks, a championship would mean three titles in sixty-five years, roughly one every twenty-two years in a thirty-team league. Even without a win this season, they currently sit at one title every thirty-two years, almost exactly what probability would predict.

Now consider the Dodgers. They've won nine championships between Brooklyn and Los Angeles, but the franchise beginning dates back to 1883, 142 years ago. Their first title didn't arrive until year 72. If you were a Dodgers fan in the late nineteenth or early twentieth century, there's a good chance you lived your entire life without seeing your team win it all.

So why do we associate the Dodgers with success and the Mets with failure? Much of it comes down to recency bias, the powerful tendency to overweight recent experiences when forming judgments, even when long-term data tells a quite different story.

In sports, the collateral damage of recency bias is usually limited to impatient general managers or coaches getting fired too quickly, as evidenced by the number of high-caliber NFL coaches dismissed each year. But in investing, the consequences are far more serious.

Recency bias causes investors to overweight market downturns and bull runs alike, particularly those individuals with long time horizons who should benefit most from patience. Sensational headlines generate clicks and revenue for publishers, but they also trigger emotionally driven decisions at precisely the wrong moments. "Buy high and sell low" may sound like a joke, but behavioral finance shows it's often closer to reality than parody.

Just as a single losing streak doesn't define a franchise, a bad year, or even a bad market cycle, doesn't define a long-term investment plan. Yet our instincts push us to rewrite the story every time the scoreboard changes. The real edge, in both sports fandom and investing, isn't prediction; it's perspective. Championships and compounding alike reward patience, discipline, and the ability to resist letting the most recent outcome outweigh the much longer game being played.

The concept of the scarcity effect isn't technically a type of bias, but when it's not a chronic orientation, it has a similar effect on our daily decisions.

Recently, my wife and her friend drove forty-five minutes to a one-hundred-thousand-square-foot book warehouse that had no air-conditioning on one of the hottest days of the year. Politely questioning the logic of that, I was informed that this warehouse is only open to the public one weekend per month, and all books are 70 percent off the list price! If you aren't familiar with retail pricing, the general rule of thumb involves a concept called "keystone" pricing. If something costs $40 at retail, then the wholesaler sells it to the retailer for $20 and the manufacturer sells it to the wholesaler for

$10. So, even at 70 percent off, the owners of the warehouse were probably still profitable.

Guessing here, but I would say my wife returned home with about twenty books. I had assumed the books would be many years out of print, but although they weren't new releases, most were published within the last couple of years. Knowing that Sunday was the last day to shop for these great deals for another month, we went back the next day where I proudly hauled in fourteen books of my own for a very reasonable cost of $74! While waiting in an exceptionally long line, I chatted with the couple in front of us who had brought their own wagon to fill with books. I mentioned how long the line was and they told me it was even longer last month! That got me thinking—how much do these folks read? Are they really reading an entire wagon of books each month, or does the scarcity effect cause them to buy more than they normally would?

Believing the latter and not the former, it got me thinking of other similar, but less dramatic, examples of this concept of scarcity. Do professors see more students outside of class by posting office hours versus having an "open door" policy? Does Chik-fil-A make more revenue each week by closing on Sundays versus being open seven days a week?

For our 401(k) advisory team we proudly tell prospective clients that "your employees will have 100 percent access to our team at all times." Hoping to prepare as many of our clients' employees for a dignified retirement as we can, we think that one-on-one customized advice is a great way to do that. But perhaps we're wrong? Would we be able to make a larger impact on 401(k) participants by creating specific windows of time that our team members are available? A small, unscientific sampling is when we do in-person enrollment meetings. Anecdotally, it seems to me like we get better attendance when we offer fewer sessions versus many meetings throughout the day. I'm not quite ready to change our value proposition just yet, but I'm going to monitor it a little more closely!

Some good examples of confirmation bias? Just look around. It's everywhere, whether you realize it at the time or not.

Artificial intelligence is still in its infancy, and yet it has already accomplished a great deal when it comes to improving productivity. Unfortunately, it has also ruined a few things along the way, and I'm not even going to get into this new AI dating trend I keep hearing about.

Long before you could alter a video on the internet to magically make dogs and cats speak like humans, you had to watch pet owners' home videos featuring what they insisted were their furry friends talking to them. Don't believe me? Watch three *America's Funniest Home Videos* reruns in a row and tell me you didn't see at least one segment devoted to this "phenomenon." Or spend fifteen minutes of your life you'll never get back scrolling through your Facebook feed.

Sorry to be the one to tell you this, but … they aren't really talking. And trust me about this because I constantly try to convince my wife that our rescue dogs, Romeo and Juliet, have these same magical abilities. If you listen to our Chihuahua mix combine howling and barking, on a regular basis, it sounds a lot like "I love you." And this isn't the first time I was certain my pets were unique. I spent most of my childhood believing our family beagle could say both "out" when he stood by the door and "Milk-Bone" while staring at the pantry.

People hear what they want to hear, and when it comes to talking dogs or singing cats, this form of confirmation bias is harmless. When they focus on the few sounds that seem meaningful and ignore the many that clearly aren't, it makes for a few good laughs. But when confirmation bias presents itself in the world of finance, it can come with far greater consequences.

A recent example of a cocktail party topic that has cooled off quite a bit lately is the infatuation with cryptocurrency, and specifically Bitcoin. As of this writing, it's down nearly 50 percent from its all-time high, and unfortunately there are many speculators who bought at the top and now need to decide whether to get out or continue its wild ride. I take no pleasure in the fact that I've cautioned clients and friends against crypto as an investment strategy, but the reality is that I don't personally invest in things I don't understand.

And when it comes to Bitcoin, although I understand the mechanics behind the transactions, I also know that it doesn't have an underlying asset that backs its value. Gold's value is attributed to the physical precious metal, and the US dollar is backed by the taxing authority of the United States government.

Do you know anyone who has ever done research on a vacation home they wanted to buy? A classic or antique car? I once spent three hours with a relative who wanted to move from the Midwest to Florida and asked for my advice. He shared materials from a presentation he had attended; a relatively unknown builder was developing a neighborhood in a rural town ninety minutes from the closest major city. In addition to the homes being built, they promised golf courses, shopping centers, medical facilities, and much more. I suggested there were areas of Florida already developed at a similar price point and closer to family members who already lived in the state.

I didn't quite understand why the conversation went on for so long. I was clear in my opinion that taking a chance on a community still in the idea phase presented plenty of risks. Our conversation ended with my relative saying, "Well, I'm sorry you feel that way. I signed the contract this morning with the builder."

And there it was—our meeting wasn't about gathering opinions. It was about getting me to agree that his decision was a good one.

Confirmation bias isn't a character flaw; it's a human one. We all want reassurance that the choices we've made and the beliefs we hold are the right ones. Hearing "I love you" in a dog's howl is harmless and even endearing. But in investing and major financial decisions, the cost of hearing only what we want to hear can be very real. The discipline isn't in being right all the time; it's in being willing to look for the evidence that might prove us wrong.

At least once a month, I notice a new "Little Free Library" pop up somewhere in town. I've seen so many that I finally decided to learn more about their mission. What I discovered was remarkable: These small book–exchange boxes now form a global network of more than two hundred thousand libraries, expanding access to books in communities around the world.

I've occasionally contributed by dropping in a book or two and have certainly borrowed titles I might never have picked up otherwise. What fascinates me most, though, is how these birdhouse-shaped kiosks illustrate, perhaps unintentionally, the concept of the "paradox of choice," popularized in 2004 by author and TED speaker Barry Schwartz.

The idea is simple: When people are given too many options, decision-making becomes stressful, even paralyzing. Long before Schwartz published *The Paradox of Choice: Why More Is Less*, I heard this described as the "Baskin Robbins Effect." Despite offering thirty-one flavors, one of the brand's perennial bestsellers is plain Vanilla. Surprising? Maybe not. Faced with Rocky Road, Twix Caramel Crunch, and dozens of other tempting choices, many people retreat to the safe and familiar.

That's the beauty of the Little Free Library. In just a few minutes, you can exchange your latest read for one of roughly twenty books and be on your way. Compared with navigating the shelves of a full-size public library, it can take longer just to get inside the building than it does to select a good read at one of these kiosks.

The same principle applies well beyond books and ice cream counters, especially in retirement plans. Every day, my team reviews company 401(k) investment menus as part of our advisory work. More often than not, the majority of plan assets are concentrated in just a few mutual funds. In fact, the more funds a plan offers, the narrower the actual spread of assets tends to be.

Financial advice is never a one-size-fits-all solution, and there may be valid reasons for a company to include forty, fifty, or even sixty funds in its retirement plan. But regardless of the number of options, someone always carries the fiduciary responsibility to prudently select, monitor, and, if necessary, replace the plan's investments. As the paradox of choice reminds us, expanding the menu can unintentionally dilute the very benefit employers hope to provide.

Even outside of finance, we all face moments when we present choices to others—a vacation destination, a restaurant for date night, or which series to binge-watch. Next time, try offering fewer options and see how it works. Sometimes, less truly is more.

And if you're ever faced with a choice between Vanilla and Twix Caramel Crunch, go with the latter. You won't be disappointed.

CHAPTER 4

THE KIDS ARE MORE THAN ALL RIGHT

As mentioned earlier, I'm a New York Mets fan. Yes, I know, please don't feel sorry for me. On Sunday home games, the Mets host special Kids Club events for young fans. When the games are televised, a few select children get to trot out to the field to meet their favorite player before the first pitch. In some cases, we get to hear the interaction between the two. The player will typically ask the young fan what their favorite ice cream flavor is, do they have any pets, and other questions, such as, "If you had a superpower, what would it be?" Definitely a fun way to start the game.

One day every year we also get to see a special event in which two Major League Baseball teams travel to Williamsport, Pennsylvania, to play a night game in front of twenty teams that qualified for the Little League World Series. One recent memorable year was the Mets vs. the Mariners. Although it has a different format than Sunday Kids Day at Citi Field, the players still get a chance to interact with the children, and I was expecting more of the same line of questions.

It shouldn't come as a surprise that the answer to, "What do you want to do when you grow up?" was, "Be a professional baseball player." But ... the follow-up question was better, and the response was classic. "What are you doing to make that happen?" Those questions stuck with me because they apply far beyond baseball. Without hesitating, the twelve-year-old articulated the training and sacrifices that would be necessary to attain his goals. You have heard that hope is not a strategy, but dreams are just hopes in disguise, with little substance to back them up. This young athlete was prepared for the question more so than most adults would be, and many of us have never been on camera in front of an audience of millions.

Our advisory team has interacted with thousands of 401(k) participants over our careers. We often use sixty-five years old as the target retirement date during a one-on-one conversation; however, it's not uncommon for us to hear someone tell us that they want to retire earlier. It's easy to pull up retirement calculators and simulate different scenarios based on deferral percentages, employer contributions, rates of return, as well as safe rates of withdrawals during retirement. Although contributing to a 401(k) account is a large part of what someone needs to do to prepare for an early retirement, there are many other variables to weigh for that goal to become a reality. Current spending, borrowing habits, charitable giving, and savings outside the retirement plan are just a few factors to consider.

So, the next time I hear a participant say they want to retire early, I'm going to pause on the calculator and instead ask them, "Outside of the 401(k), what are you doing to make that happen?" I'm hopeful this will be a great foundation for the conversation so that we include all financial decisions and behaviors when outlining a path for success.

Oh, and by the way, former New York Mets player Todd Frazier led Toms River East to the 1998 Little League World Series title by hitting four home runs during the tournament and striking out the last batter to secure the win. Like Frazier, anyone striving for an ambitious goal needs to do more than simply dream. They need a plan and daily actions to back it up.

———

Knowing that discipline, focus, and drive are established at a young age, I often ask a job candidate to reflect on the years that preceded the first entry on their highly curated résumé.

Over the course of my leadership career, I recruited, interviewed, hired, and onboarded dozens, if not hundreds, of sales representatives. As I moved into larger organizations, the process became increasingly structured and well supported. With those resources came clarity: Few responsibilities matter more to a sales leader than getting the right people in the room.

Large corporations often assign talent acquisition specialists, internal recruiters who typically report through human resources, to support middle and senior management. That was my experience toward the end of my corporate career. Year after year, I unsuccessfully advocated for those recruiters to be embedded within the sales organization.

My reasoning was simple. Recruiting is selling. In competitive labor markets, attracting top candidates requires persuasion, credibility, and follow-through, the same skills needed to win business. Just as important, I wanted recruiters' incentives aligned with long-term outcomes. When compensation is tied only to placement and not performance, accountability fades.

Before recruiting was fully insourced, local managers were often permitted to work with external firms. I rarely negotiated fees aggressively, but I focused heavily on replacement guarantees. Even then, the ultimate responsibility for building a strong team never left the sales manager's desk.

Earlier in my career, before internal recruiters and before third-party firms were an option, hiring fell entirely on the sales manager. I was fortunate to have strong mentors during that period, and their guidance shaped how I evaluated talent long before résumés were filtered by software or process.

The mechanics of résumé review are easy to learn. Look for careless errors. Be cautious of candidates who change jobs every two years, often the amount of time it takes to manage out a poor performer. In sales, look for evidence of goal setting and measurable achievement.

Athletic backgrounds often provide an early signal. Both team and individual athletes spend years setting goals, competing, and learning to manage success and failure.

One mentor pushed me to look more closely at candidates from individual sports. During one conversation, she described a hire she had made years earlier: a woman with no sales experience but a long history as a competitive youth figure skater, beginning at age six and continuing through her early teens.

Her interview questions were unconventional. "How big was your hometown?" "How many ice rinks did you have?" In many parts of Connecticut, the answers were predictable—small towns, one rink. That led to the defining question: "What time did you practice each day?"

In small towns with a single rink, ice time runs around the clock during the winter and is allocated by age and sport. High school hockey teams get the desirable after-school hours. Young figure skaters are left with what remains, often between three and six in the morning.

Figure skating alone doesn't predict success. But showing up at those hours, year after year, reveals something more important: resilience. It also signals a strong support system. A child that age isn't driving herself to the rink. There are parents making sacrifices alongside her.

The lesson was not to hire only figure skaters from small towns. The lesson was to look at things differently. To move beyond surface credentials and search for evidence of discipline, commitment, and sustained effort. Don't aim to slightly outperform the industry's typical 30 to 40 percent annual sales turnover. Eliminate it. Less time spent on recruiting and replacing people means that there is more time available to develop them.

With that mindset, I hired beauty pageant winners, wrestlers, marathon runners, and candidates with traditional sales backgrounds alike.

Some of my most successful hires came from unlikely places. One was a rental car company with a management training program for recent graduates. Trainees wore suits and ties and then washed returned cars in those same clothes. Another was a book company that hired college students to sell door-to-door in towns they had never lived in: twelve weeks of cold-calling, commission-only pay, and evenings spent alone in short-term rentals with no social network.

My question to those candidates was always the same: "Did you come back the next summer and do it again?"

If the answer was yes, the rest of the interview was unnecessary. The offer was the easy part.

Strong hiring decisions are rarely driven by credentials alone. They come from recognizing patterns of discipline, resilience, and long-term commitment, often revealed in places most managers never think to look. When leaders hire for capacity and character rather than convenience, turnover declines, development accelerates, and leadership shifts from constant replacement to sustained growth.

As a financial advisor specializing in 401(k) retirement plans, one of the benefits of my work is the opportunity to meet with people from many diverse backgrounds. Since launching our advisory firm, our primary goal has been to help as many individuals as we can prepare for a dignified and meaningful retirement. A recent study showed that approximately 94 percent of participants in our 401(k) plans had never met with, or even had access to, a financial advisor prior to our engagement.

In addition to the work we are compensated for, I also participate in the CFP® Board's Pro Bono Challenge. The purpose of this initiative is to help people take control of their financial lives and to have a positive impact on individuals, families, and communities. Recently, I had the pleasure of committing one of those pro bono hours to a planning meeting with a twenty-one-year-old college student currently working in the fast-casual food industry. I'm always hopeful I can add value during these meetings, but the reality is that I often walk away feeling like I gained just as much, if not more, than the person I'm helping.

To protect her identity, I'll call our young saver "Kelly." Kelly is doing all the right things financially. She only buys used cars, maintains an emergency savings account equal to three months of pay in a high-yield interest account, and already understands two of the most important principles in investing: delayed gratification and the power of compounding.

Halfway through the meeting, I didn't know whether to continue guiding her or offer her a job. We then began discussing her 401(k). The company she works for offers a generous employer matching contribution of 100 percent up to 4 percent of her pay. She immediately let me know she was taking full advantage of the match by deferring 4 percent. As I do in most meetings, I encouraged her to consider increasing her deferral percentage. Kelly was adamant that 4 percent was all she could afford and, based on how in tune she was with her finances, I didn't push back.

Since we were meeting over Zoom, I suggested we log into her 401(k) account for a quick review. Kelly was surprised to see that her deferral percentage was set to 7 percent. How could that be? A quick review of her plan highlights revealed the answer: Her plan includes an auto-enroll/auto-increase feature. Three years ago, she was auto-enrolled at 4 percent, and, unbeknownst to her, the auto-increase of 1 percent per year had raised her contribution to the current 7 percent. I won't bore you with math but suffice it to say that her 401(k) balance was substantially higher than it would have been had she remained at 4 percent. Extrapolate that growth to a retirement age of sixty-five, and it's reasonable to conclude that this feature will have a dramatic impact on her retirement nest egg and her future lifestyle.

Every day, we speak with plan participants about asset allocation, Roth versus Traditional contributions, beneficiary elections, and a dozen other common themes. I am increasingly convinced that one of the most important actions anyone can take is to either elect, or avoid disabling, the auto-increase feature in their 401(k) plan. Increasing contributions by 1 to 2 percent per year, with a reasonable cap of 15 percent, is a complete game changer for retirement savings.

Going away to college is usually the first time a teenager will have the freedom to make many of their own decisions without a parent's influence. Of course, having autonomy each day to decide between studying and partying may explain why the dropout rates are the highest during freshman year.

Recently, I was fortunate to be invited to attend the "Future Advisors Conference" at the University of Florida, an event designed to introduce students majoring in Finance with a minor in Wealth Management to advisory firms for internships.

Having no children of my own, and approaching six decades on this planet, I was concerned there might be too large a generational gap for me to relate to these young, ambitious people. I half-expected eye rolls when I spoke to these aspiring advisors, with whispers of, "Okay, boomer, that's not how things work anymore." Instead, I got just the opposite.

The conference kicked off with a reception at the on-campus football stadium. What a fantastic way to create a casual atmosphere while highlighting a culture of excellence through UF athletics. "Meet us at the Heisman Trophy Display Case by Gate 1," the invitation read. Most schools have never had a Heisman Trophy winner, awarded to the best player in college football each year, but the Gators have had three.

Coming straight from work, I already had my suit on, but, worried that I might be overdressed, I loosened my tie. That changed quickly once the elevator doors opened to the luxury boxes where the event was being held. The young men and women were dressed professionally and looked like it wasn't their first time. I'm fairly sure I didn't own a suit in college, and even if I had, I doubt I would have worn it to a football stadium.

Not one student was staring at their feet or scrolling on their phone, a common criticism of Gen Z. News flash: Go to any airport gate and you'll see it's the older travelers who are glued to their mobile devices. Don't let the facts get in the way of a good story.

Fast-forward to the next morning. Knowing I'd be sitting in an uncomfortable ballroom chair most of the day, I decided to squeeze in a quick workout at the hotel gym before heading to the conference. I misread the agenda and thought we were starting at 8:00 a.m., but that was just when the continental breakfast began. The speakers didn't start until 8:45. I grabbed a table close to the stage, and within five minutes, six students joined me. They had already eaten and had notepads and pens in hand as they took turns introducing themselves.

What followed absolutely blew me away. We spent the next thirty minutes in a roundtable discussion about the industry, what hiring firms are looking for, and how they could best prepare for a career in this field. These were mostly sophomores. Every one of them took notes during our impromptu session, and not one monopolized the conversation. Each took their turn asking thoughtful questions.

The day continued to improve as each speaker focused on their area of expertise. I was especially encouraged to hear several of the speakers reinforce the points we discussed that morning, occasionally accompanied by a shoulder tap or a smile from one of my six new friends. The day wrapped up with each student asking for my business card, and by that evening all six had sent a LinkedIn connection request. A few even followed up with an email.

If you're concerned about this generation's focus or drive...don't be. And even though I'm a South Carolina Gamecock, you can be certain one of these young superstars will end up on my advisory team someday.

CHAPTER 5

LEADERSHIP REDEFINED: LESSONS YOU WON'T LEARN IN BUSINESS SCHOOL

Young sales leaders learn early that the ability to recruit, select, train, and develop talented sales representatives is the single strongest predictor of their success.

In *Good to Great*, Jim Collins writes about making sure you have employees in the right seat on the bus and even making sure they're on the right bus to begin with. This metaphor is about optimizing the unique talents everyone possesses while also confirming that they represent the professional and cultural standards of your organization.

As mentioned in the previous chapter, when leading sales teams, I knew I needed to be creative in sourcing talent rather than relying solely on the traditional recruiting channels my competitors used. Many candidates came through family and friends. The character of these job seekers usually wasn't an issue, since most of my personal network shared values similar to my own. The most difficult moments came when the fit wasn't there, because it sometimes felt personal to tell both the applicant and the referral source that we wouldn't be moving forward.

In some cases, I took a chance. When I was a younger manager, my ego was still inflated enough to believe I could coach anyone into a successful sales career. On one occasion, I hired a friend's spouse. Christine was interested in a career change and felt her pay as a teacher didn't properly reflect the effort that profession required. It's not much of a stretch for teachers to move into sales, so I took the risk, hoping I could provide the platform for her to begin realizing her true worth.

It didn't work.

Although completely unscientific, we estimated that the strength of our brand and the national reputation of our organization meant each sales territory could generate about four sales units per month on its own. At the time, the average sales representative produced ten units per month, meaning the six incremental units were the result of their prospecting and selling skills. Christine averaged only two to three sales per month total, and after just two quarters it became clear a change was needed. Christine was actually the one who approached me, humbly admitting she wasn't enjoying herself.

I was certain about two things. First, her effort was there but call reluctance and a lack of assertiveness would continue to hold her back. Second, she was absolutely on the right bus.

I asked for two weeks to figure it out, and Christine agreed. Our branch manager oversaw all operations in the market, so I went straight from my meeting with Christine into his office to see if he had any openings on the service team, keeping my intentions somewhat vague.

"Nope, we're fully staffed," Tim said almost immediately.

Disappointed, I asked if he had any suggestions for helping me find the right seat within the company for Christine.

"Christine? Of course, we'll take her!" he said excitedly. He would get permission to over-hire, and he looked like he had just won the lottery.

However, whether fair or not, working on the sales side of the house typically comes with higher compensation. The pay difference is often justified by the variable nature of commissions and the higher turnover risk that comes with quota-carrying roles. So, although we had found the right seat on the bus for Christine, I also needed to explain there would be a significant decrease in pay.

"I'll take it," she said on the spot, even after hearing the salary adjustment.

That was more than thirty years ago. Today, Christine is a senior leader in the Service Department. She runs one of the largest markets in the entire organization and has developed and promoted hundreds of team members over three decades of excellence. I consider this one of the greatest hiring success stories of my career.

Sometimes the real win isn't coaching someone harder; it's positioning them better. When leaders focus on getting the right people on the bus and then work just as hard to find them the right seat, both the individual and the organization benefit.

Recruiting is hard, but it's just the beginning. Before you could screen résumés electronically, the manual process of sorting through hundreds of documents was cumbersome at best. To identify those that were invited to formally enter the interview process, you would apply a few knockout factors first to make the list more manageable. As mentioned previously, quickly eliminating spelling errors, job hoppers, and inflated works of fiction would usually produce a list of semifinalists for in-person meetings.

A mentor once told me that interviews should begin when the candidate walks into the building, not when they sit across from you in an office or conference room. Getting feedback from the receptionist on how a candidate speaks and behaves upon arrival is invaluable.

For a business-to-business outside sales representative, there are dozens of these "front-of-the-house" interactions each week with prospective clients, often without knowing how much influence they may have on the final decision. In small businesses, the receptionist is frequently a family member of the owner—being dismissive toward them can be fatal to any potential sale. More importantly, treating anyone disrespectfully is a character flaw that doesn't belong in any organization.

I took this idea a step further and believed the interview began when the candidate pulled into our parking lot. As a new manager, I didn't have the best office location—no greenery, no pond, no Zen garden, just a giant parking lot near the front door. Over the years, I was offered upgrades, but I usually declined because I didn't want to give up my front-row seat to candidates' arrivals.

So, what was I looking for? Or, more importantly, what did I hope not to see? In my ideal world, a candidate arrived ten minutes early, exited the car fully put together, walked briskly but calmly, and entered the building without drama. What I often saw instead were candidates arriving with one minute to spare, speeding into the lot, finishing their outfits in the car, and using tinted windows as mirrors for last-minute grooming. Those interviews didn't last long.

Assuming they passed the parking lot test, the next screening, unbeknownst to them, was their interaction with the receptionist. Starbucks gift cards made excellent compensation for my friends up front in exchange for jotting down answers to a few questions and discreetly passing them to my assistant: How did they greet you? Did they make eye contact? Did they ask your name? Did they introduce themselves and explain why they were there without being prompted?

It sounds basic, yet, surprisingly, many failed this amazingly easy test. Instead, I'd hear that the candidate checked their notes to remember who to ask for, made better eye contact with their phone than the receptionist, or spent their time in the lobby cramming at the last minute.

If a candidate failed one or both pre-interview tests, I still met with them. Why? Because even if I didn't think they were a fit for my team—short of being outright rude, they still deserved respect. Often, they were referred by someone I trusted, and there was no reason to damage that relationship.

I could write an entire book about the actual interview itself, but to keep things pithy, I'll share one answer that nearly cost a candidate a job, a candidate who later became my top performer and even finished first in the entire organization in sales one year.

"What was your GPA in college?" I asked. Every corporate training session had told me this was a bad question and that I should stick to behavioral interviewing. I didn't always follow the script.

"It was like a 3.0," Kevin said.

Anyone who went to college knows you want the "3 handle," not a 2.9, if you can help it. My assumption was that "like a 3.0" probably meant "not a 3.0." I pushed back and asked whether it was actually a 3.0 or higher, or not. He clarified, "Yes, it was a 3.0." Kevin checked every other box, but I couldn't let it go. If he was embellishing here, would he exaggerate once he had the job?

So, I proposed a simple solution: Go to the registrar's office and bring me an official transcript. If it was a 3.0 or higher, he'd get the offer. If it was a 2.9 or below, we'd part ways. He accepted the challenge, and learned a lesson, though probably not the one you'd expect.

If you think it was "don't embellish your GPA—it can be verified," you'd be wrong. Instead, it was "make sure you pay your parking tickets before you graduate."

The registrar thanked him for stopping by and told him his transcript would be waiting once he brought a check for $324 to cover unpaid parking violations. He did, drove straight to my office, and handed me the transcript. His GPA? A 3.05. I kept my word, extended the offer, and he accepted on the spot.

The lesson in all of this is simple: Interviews never begin, or end, when we think they do. How someone treats strangers, prepares for small moments, and handles uncomfortable accountability reveals far more than rehearsed answers ever could. Talent can be trained, but character is harder to coach, and in sales, where trust is currency, character is often the difference between a good hire and a great one.

Kevin experienced success almost immediately, but Michael's career started off on very shaky ground.

The need for work-life balance is a real thing. However, thirty years ago it wasn't something you talked to your boss about. Want to climb the corporate ladder at record speed? The real high achievers knew implicitly that being a workaholic would get you to your goals faster. Sometimes it was even explicit. I once had a manager tell me that he was a strong supporter of work-life balance. I heard him tell an employee that when they're in the office, he wants them to focus on work, and when they get home after 7:00 p.m., they can focus on life. "See, there's your balance," he said with a straight face.

Back in the nineties, I was part of the problem, not the solution, when it came to employees wanting to be well-rounded. My team sales meetings started at 7:30 a.m. sharp each Monday morning, and it was widely known that I believed if you weren't ten minutes early for a meeting, you would be late. The door to the conference room shut right on time, and if you didn't want to be shamed into explaining your tardiness to the group, you made sure you were on the correct side of that door.

As a young manager in my twenties with no children and few responsibilities outside of work, it's not too surprising that I scored close to zero on empathy when taking leadership profile assessments. But one event on a snowy February morning allowed me to soften my rigid policy.

My newest recruit lived forty-five minutes from the office, and I was reluctant to offer him the job because of the distance. There was no virtual working back then; sales cases were submitted in person on paper at the office, so windshield time had a direct impact on sales reps' productivity.

During the final interview, when I presented the offer letter to Michael, I made him aware of my nonnegotiables, and being punctual was at the top of the list. So, it was hard for me to focus on the agenda when, on his first day, Michael showed up twelve minutes late, knocking on the locked conference room door at 7:42 a.m.

"Welcome, Michael—let's make sure we grab some time together right after the meeting."

My team didn't bother introducing themselves, assuming this would be both his first and last day on the job.

I had just finished some leadership training on the art of "being curious," so while walking back to my office with Michael after the meeting, I asked in a nonjudgmental way what caused his delayed arrival.

"I'm sorry—it won't happen again," Michael apologetically offered.

I needed Michael more than he knew, as I had the toughest time filling the territory covering the northeast corner of Connecticut. Finding an experienced sales professional who not only lived there but also had an extensive network was difficult, to say the least, and Michael checked those boxes.

Listening wasn't my strongest attribute at that point in my career, so I offered him an immediate life lesson.

"Here's some advice, Michael. If you want to ensure you're on time for something, build in a big buffer, especially for your first day on the job. Leave early and find a nice coffee shop nearby if you show up too early."

And then came the story that not even Hollywood could make up.

"Well, that was the plan, sir," Michael began to explain. "I left home in time to arrive ninety minutes early. It was still dark and snowing hard. About two miles from my house, I started thinking about how excited I was about this opportunity, and what a beautiful snowy morning it was in our little rural town. I looked to my left and saw this handsome horse running through the snow, completely free and seemingly enjoying the fresh powder. My happiness turned to fear as I realized that horse was mine, and he had broken through our gate. I must not have secured the latch when I checked on him earlier in the morning.

"I pulled my car over to the side, and even though I had a suit and dress shoes on, I knew I needed to chase him down and get him back to the barn. Fortunately, I was successful and walked him back home two miles, this time double-checking the latch to make sure it was secure. Too embarrassed to tell my wife, and knowing she was getting our two young daughters ready for school, I couldn't ask her for a ride back to my car. So, I picked up my pace to a slight jog, still in work shoes, and made it back to my car. The rest of the trip to Hartford was uneventful, and like I said, boss, I'm sorry I was twelve minutes late, and it won't happen again."

I've had the pleasure of coaching multiple sales teams during my career, and twice I was fortunate to have the number one sales representative in the organization on my team. Michael ascended to that position in just his second full fiscal year, in a territory that had barely produced any new clients up to that point.

That snowy morning taught me a leadership lesson no training program ever could: Policies may be black and white, but people are far more complex. Punctuality still matters, and standards still have a place, but so do curiosity, context, and a willingness to listen before judging. Sometimes the difference between losing a great employee and developing a star performer is simply the decision to pause long enough to understand the story behind the behavior.

CHAPTER 6

LEADERSHIP REDEFINED II: WHEN LEADERSHIP GETS REAL

Having finally decided that I wanted to turn my personal finance hobby into a career, I gathered enough courage to walk into the local office of the brokerage firm that held my investment accounts to request a meeting with the branch manager. Cold-calling a Wall Street establishment to ask for a job certainly wasn't the norm, and my résumé didn't highlight any advanced degrees from Ivy League schools. I needed an angle to make sure that the resident director would take the meeting, so when asked by the receptionist about the purpose of my visit, I told her that I wanted to change the financial advisor for my account.

Although it should have been obvious to me at the time, requesting to "fire" your financial advisor, regardless of account size, got the attention of leadership. I would also later learn that, although this makes no sense, even worse than taking your business to another brokerage firm was asking for a new advisor in the same office. Pride trumps logic.

As I sat down in the well-appointed corner office with a mahogany desk and leather-upholstered chairs, he got straight to business. "I'm sorry that your current advisor hasn't met your needs, but I'm hopeful that I can provide you with a solution," the busy executive began. I was immediately impressed with the "sad but glad" statement, always a good way to defuse a potential client issue. "Do you have a specific advisor in mind that you'd like to move your accounts to?" he continued. He was confused when I requested Bob Darrow as my advisor. "Sorry, but we don't have anyone by that name that works in this office—could he possibly report to a different branch?"

It was then that I realized I had failed to tell him my name. He was even more perplexed when I informed him that I was Bob Darrow. "Well, you're not employed here, so I'm not sure how that would really work." "Yes, but if you hire me into your training program," I exclaimed, "I'll be my own first client."

What I didn't know at the time was that the firm had just started a rapid expansion of their training program. They were willing to hire unlicensed candidates with different backgrounds, sponsor them for their securities exams, and invest heavily in their development. More rapidly than I ever expected, the director fast-tracked me through their pre-hire assessments and thorough interview process, resulting in a job offer within a week.

I knew that I had to accept the offer since this was the best scenario I could have imagined that allowed me to turn my passion into a vocation. Because I had spent my entire fourteen-year professional career with the same company, I wanted to make sure that I left on good terms. My new employer was kind enough to let me give more than the standard two weeks' notice so that I could ensure my sales territory was fully covered and that I could introduce my successor to my clients and referral sources. I would learn six years later that leaving in good standing allowed me to return to that same company. Having coasted to the finish line may have prevented me from becoming a rehire.

We have a phrase when employees "limp" through the finish line versus finishing on a high note—it's called "quiet quitting," and there was no way that I would allow myself to be included in that group.

Because sometimes the most valuable thing you can do for your future career is give full effort to a job you're already leaving.

What began as false bravado quickly morphed into impostor syndrome after my first day on the job. In the back of my mind, I had this illogical fear that I would show up for work one morning and they'd say something to the effect of, "Okay, we're on to you. You really don't belong here, do you?"

New advisors are given twenty-four months to graduate from the training program. Graduation was a really nice way of saying that you would no longer have a base salary guaranteed by the firm. Assuming you have gathered enough assets, your book of business should now sustain your income moving forward.

I was fortunate to have the probationary tag removed in just ten months, but during that first year, I learned more about people than I did about finance.

You can discard about 99 percent of what you see in movies that portray the financial services industry as some kind of boiler-room business filled with endless debauchery. I never witnessed fast-talking salespeople yelling "Buy! Sell!" at the top of their lungs, nor was I ever invited to the kind of parties portrayed in *The Wolf of Wall Street*.

There were, however, individuals who would easily fail the litmus test of "would you invite them to your home for dinner?"

There are many kinds of financial advisory firms. Some are insurance-based, and many are referred to as "fee-only" fiduciaries. In the early part of the twenty-first century, however, most firms had commission-based advisors, meaning a significant percentage of the advisor's pay came from recommending products to their clients.

Whether it was a mutual fund, annuity, or retirement plan platform, each of the companies that distributed products through these firms employed wholesalers. The wholesaler's role was to go from office to office, through either scheduled meetings or by "walking the floor," to explain why their offering should be positioned above their competitors.

These salespeople leveraged their time by holding "lunch and learns," taking eight to ten advisors out for a meal in exchange for a fifteen-minute commercial at the end of lunch.

Early on, I noticed that there were advisors who went to lunch with no intention of doing business with the vendor, barely paying attention during the presentation. More appalling was when the server discreetly handed a take-home bag to one of these plate lickers, knowing the unscrupulous broker had just secured his dinner for the evening as well.

I shared my disbelief with the top advisor in the office, and he gave me advice I have carried with me throughout my career.

First, he said, don't ever go to a "lunch and learn." Ever. The value of your time far exceeds the cost of the meal being provided. Second, the only reason to do business with that individual is if they offer the best product for your clients' needs. He said that while this may sound obvious, your judgment can be subliminally skewed into feeling as if you owe something for that free lunch. Finally, he said, if you genuinely want to hear about the features and benefits of the product, the best place to do that is in your office, not in a noisy restaurant.

This all made tons of sense.

One problem: I didn't have an office yet.

Newbies were relegated to the bullpen—rows of cubicles with no privacy—making it difficult to concentrate, much less conduct a business meeting. That was easily solved by grabbing one of the conference rooms, an option I offered many of the wholesalers who wanted to meet.

Interestingly, there were a couple of wholesalers who told me they preferred to meet me in my tiny, uncomfortable, and certainly not made-for-two workstation.

This made no sense.

And then, one day, it dawned on me.

My guest chair had a perfect view of the number one advisor's office, allowing them to cut my meeting short the moment that advisor got off the phone.

It was a small moment, but it stuck with me. In business, and in leadership, people rarely tell you about their real motivation. They show it. The leaders who thrive aren't the ones who take everything at face value. They're the ones who learn to read the room, question the free lunch, and pay attention to where the chair is actually facing.

I quietly quit golf a few months ago, forgetting to tell my weekend foursome that the passion just wasn't there anymore. I still showed up, but they weren't getting my best effort. The problem with quiet quitting is that it's rarely as quiet as the person doing it thinks.

As a senior leader, I was always surprised when a manager would call in shock to tell me a sales rep had given notice. "That came out of nowhere," they'd say, a line I heard more times than I can count.

Talented salespeople are the number one predictor of success, but being short-staffed for long stretches is a death sentence for a sales leader. Fortunately, it doesn't have to be that way. Let's look at this from both a left-brain, analytical lens and a right-brain, people-first one.

Assuming leadership and HR don't over-constrain hiring, simple math can keep a team close to full productivity year-round. I've worked in environments where managers weren't allowed to hire until someone left. Those executives didn't last long, and rightly so. That level of short-term thinking has no place in a growing organization.

Optimally, a manager should lead six to eight reps. Reality often stretches that to ten or more in the name of cost control. I once had seventeen direct reports, and while that was hard on me, it was worse for them. With that span of control, there's barely time for anything beyond approvals and reviews. Development? Coaching? Not happening.

Let's use eight reps as our example. Industry turnover in outside B2B sales runs about 30 to 35 percent annually, meaning you'll need to hire roughly three new reps each year. This was one of the first conversations I had when taking over teams as a director. Managers, understandably loyal and optimistic, would walk me through every rep and explain why none of them were at risk. The math rarely agreed.

Factor in ramp time, say three months of training and another three to reach full productivity, and you're six months out before a new hire contributes meaningfully. Without getting overly granular, this means you'll need one or two reps to significantly outperform quota each year. In a healthy system, you hire every four months, train continuously, and are always within a month of your next start date. In other words: You're always hiring, and you always have an opening.

Unfortunately, most sales leaders were top-performing reps, and top reps tend to be right-brained, relationship-driven, intuitive, and instinctive. You won't usually find a spreadsheet tracking turnover probabilities. You'll find gut feel.

So how do you spot quiet quitters before the resignation email lands? With no empirical data to support this, I'd say most employees mentally quit about three months before they formally resign. The signs aren't loud, but they're there.

They stop showing up to celebrations, happy hours, winner's dinners, and milestone events. They'll have good excuses, but previously, they didn't need them. Their sales may hold up for a while, but that can be misleading due to pipeline lag. The pipeline itself will become stale with older deals, fewer new opportunities, more "suspects" than prospects, and fewer closed-lost deals as they try to keep the funnel looking full.

When you see this, you must address it directly and quickly. The sooner you intervene, the better your odds of saving the employee, assuming they're worth saving. I once asked a mentor what acceptable turnover was. He said, "Zero percent—save every employee, every time." He meant it as emphasis, not literal truth. In reality, 10 to 15 percent turnover is healthy because it brings new talent into the organization, a mandate senior leadership rarely states explicitly.

If you reach someone while they're still wavering and willing to talk, you have a chance. You'll hear the standard answers, and they matter, but your job is to ask second- and third-level questions to get to the real issue.

"My base pay is too low" often means "I need to make more money." Those aren't the same thing.

"Our competitor's product is better" may mean "I need help positioning ours."

"I'm working too hard without results" often means "I need better process and efficiency."

Solve one or all of these with increased training, and you may change that rep's mind.

One word of caution: When someone leaves, don't kick dirt on them. Your remaining team is watching, and they'll assume anything negative you say about the departing rep could someday be said about them. I've used the simple "sad but glad" line: "I'm happy for Cameron if this is best for him and his family. I would've liked him to stay, but everyone's situation is unique." That said, I don't attend farewell parties, and trust me, they don't want you there anyway.

Finally, learn from it. There's an old saying that employees don't quit companies, they quit managers. That's harsh, but true enough to matter. There were certainly things you could've done differently to keep that person engaged. Without that humility, you'll repeat the same mistakes.

Quiet quitting rarely happens overnight—it's usually the end of a long, quiet drift. The best leaders don't wait for resignation emails; they build systems that anticipate turnover, cultures that surface disengagement early, and relationships strong enough to have hard conversations before it's too late. Do that well, and departures become exceptions instead of surprises, and your team stays closer to full strength, by design rather than by luck.

The words *leadership* and *management* are often used as synonyms in the business world, but just like a sports team, the leaders can often be found on the field, not just in the front office.

Early in my professional career, there were two distinct dress codes: one for client-facing employees and another for customer service team members who primarily worked behind the scenes. Although I could have dressed more casually when I was not meeting with clients, I typically kept my suit on throughout the day. It was simply easier to wear one set of clothes than to constantly take a tie on and off.

One weeknight, I was at the grocery store wearing my usual off-duty uniform—cargo shorts, a T-shirt, and a baseball cap—when I ran into a familiar face. A customer service representative from the office quite literally bumped into me. Startled, she apologized and then laughed, admitting she had almost not recognized me. She went on to say how shocked she was to see me dressed so casually.

Half-joking, I asked whether she thought I wore a suit on weekends as well. That is when she confessed that, in the office, I was known as having two personalities: "Work Bob" during business hours and "Fun Bob" outside of the office. And, she added, she had never met Fun Bob.

She meant it humorously, but the comment stayed with me. What I believed came across as professional and focused was often perceived as stoic and unapproachable. I could have dismissed this by telling myself that success requires sacrifice and that intense focus was simply part of the job. There may be some truth in that, but in hindsight, it was more likely a narrative I created to avoid addressing a personal development gap.

Fast-forward two years, when I was managing my first sales team. One of my reps always walked quickly through the office, constantly carried five or six "new client" folders, and wore a perpetual smile. The operations team knew him only as "Friendly James."

What they did not know was that many of those folders were empty, his fast pace had no real purpose, and he was well below quota in his first few months.

Curious, I finally asked him about it. "I'm practicing for when I'm successful," he said without hesitation.

He explained that this is what people often refer to as "fake it until you make it." And the smile? "Successful people are happy," he said. "So why wouldn't I be?"

Over the next several years, James went on to set multiple sales records, earned a promotion to manage his own team, and eventually moved into a senior leadership role.

It turns out I had it backward, and James had it exactly right.

I was fortunate to work for a company that allowed room for mistakes, especially those rooted in style rather than substance. And while I was paid to coach others toward success, I learned just as much from them along the way.

So, these days, you can call me "Fun Work Bob." And thanks to the rise of virtual meetings, I'm usually only dressed professionally from the chest up.

CHAPTER 7

YES, YOU ACTUALLY WILL USE THAT IN THE REAL WORLD

n 1975, President Gerald Ford signed the Metric Conversion Act into law, and his successor, Jimmy Carter, actively supported and promoted the voluntary shift toward the metric system.

They say the best time to learn a new language is as a child—the brain has greater plasticity at younger ages, and learning is more implicit than explicit at that time. Learning an entirely new system of measurements in elementary school seemed fun to me back then, but as I reflect on it now, I'm fairly sure the adults didn't feel the same way. I don't need to tell you that although some adoption of the metric system occurred, it was never fully embraced in the United States. We still see elements of it now, however. I understand what a five-hundred-milliliter bottle of water is, and a five-kilometer race means more to me now than it may have had the act never been signed.

Without extensive research, I'm going to take a leap and say that this may be where the saying "Don't worry, you won't ever use that in the real world" originated. This mantra was repeated often in school, but never loud enough for the teachers to hear. It was most effective when whispering under your breath to your classmates nearby. And as mentioned in a previous chapter about confirmation bias, it wasn't too difficult to find a peer that would agree with your declaration whenever you found a subject matter too difficult to navigate.

Something that has gone completely metric, though, is how liquor is sold. Ask anyone now what a fifth of liquor is and you are likely to be met with confusion, not knowing that a 750-milliliter bottle of spirits was once measured as a fifth of a gallon.

Rather than discussing the origins of the metric system, bourbon enthusiasts would much rather embrace a spirited debate over whether Blanton's, Eagle Rare, or Four Roses Small Batch offers the best experience for an evening with friends. Yet few would argue that any of those fine bottles rival the prestige of celebrating a special occasion with a pour from the Pappy Van Winkle collection.

Collectors will tell you that the Pappy 23-Year Kentucky Straight Bourbon and the Old Rip Van Winkle 25-Year are financially out of reach for most, but if you can find it, the Old Rip 10-Year won't necessarily deplete your retirement funds.

So, you can imagine how thrilled my European-vacation travel group was to discover Pappy Van Winkle listed on the menu at a boutique cocktail bar in Sweden last summer. Not only available, but seemingly at a shockingly affordable price. For just 11 euros, about $13, you could finish the night with a memorable toast.

It didn't seem quite right, so I did what any responsible (and perhaps not-so-popular) member of the group would do: I checked the fine print. The price was listed for "1 cl." Thanks to a quick search, I discovered that a centiliter is just over one-third of an ounce. A standard US pour of bourbon is closer to 5 cl, so suddenly that $13 price tag translated to roughly $65. Not quite the bargain it first appeared to be.

My travel companions were surprised, and slightly amused, when their historically "light" pours arrived. Fortunately, each had only ordered 1 cl, so the lesson was inexpensive. But imagine the reverse scenario: a European ordering drinks in the US without understanding American pouring standards. The outcome could be far more costly.

In fact, a friendly couple sitting next to us shared an old tale. Years ago, after advancing to the finals of the US Open, Swedish tennis legend Björn Borg reportedly ran into a Manhattan bar and shouted, "Sixes for everyone!" In Sweden, that phrase means one drink for each person, with six centiliters equaling a typical two-ounce pour. In New York, however, the bartender naturally assumed Borg was buying six drinks per person. Legendary generosity, or expensive misunderstanding? Probably the latter.

Now, whether that story is true (likely not), the message remains the same: Math gets tricky, especially when you're caught up in excitement and trying to make quick financial decisions on the fly.

In Sweden, we ended up with a tiny pour. Björn (supposedly) ended up with a massive bar tab. Neither consequence was life changing. But when the stakes are high—financial planning, retirement decisions, major life milestones—it pays to surround yourself with professionals who help ensure the numbers work out in your favor.

The ability to make quick calculations in your head can save you some money on your bar tab, but if you're planning a trip to the casino anytime soon, that skill can be even more impactful.

When I lived and worked in Connecticut many years ago, I had a colleague, recently divorced, who went to the casino every weekend. I get it. Casinos are fun, and I'd imagine that divorce isn't. On sporadic Mondays, usually two to three weeks apart, he'd enthusiastically wave me into his office to tell me about his big win. It is interesting, however, that on those other Mondays, we barely spoke. I wonder why?

His game of choice was craps, and if you've never bellied up to the craps table before, you haven't experienced one of the biggest adrenaline rushes in the entire establishment. The game of craps morphs into a team sport as the evening goes on, with almost everyone at the table cheering in unison against the house. What the casino won't tell you is that the makeshift fraternity you just joined is being intentionally used against you to tilt the odds in their favor.

Craps is the game that is highlighted the most in movies because of the action. The excitement increases as participants are required to shout out their intentions as they toss chips toward the bets farthest away from their position at the table. "Ten dollars on the hard four!" while two red chips are strategically hurled toward the boxman sitting in the middle, is a common refrain. This means that you are betting that double twos come up on the dice before any seven, or a combination of three and one, is rolled. I think it's a little harsh to call that a sucker bet, but the reality is that the house has roughly an 11 percent edge every time you make that wager.

The best bet at the table? Without writing an entire book on craps strategies, it's the one closest to you that doesn't require you to verbalize anything. Simply push chips behind your pass line bet when allowed and the casino will pay your wins out with "full odds," with neither party having an edge.

My colleague didn't lose because he didn't know how to add. He lost because he mistook excitement for advantage.

The casino's edge isn't built on complex equations. It's built on behavior. They make the worst bets the most entertaining. They turn long-shot wagers into social events. They make you shout your intentions as if conviction alone improves probability.

That lesson extends far beyond a craps table. In investing, in business, even in career decisions, we're constantly tempted by the "hard four" opportunities—the flashy plays with applause attached. Meanwhile, the quiet, disciplined, mathematically sound choices sit right in front of us.

Although understanding the size of your drink, as well as the odds returned on your bets at a casino, are fun for math geeks, quick micro calculations can serve you well in all aspects of life.

Much to my wife's frustration, when we travel to a place I've never been, I can't just take in the scenery or enjoy the newness of my experience. Instead, I like to interact with the locals and ask questions … lots of questions.

I have found that the tour guides and bus drivers will give you some information outside of their curated word tracks, but most of it is a polished presentation. Restaurant servers, bartenders, and shopkeepers—now that's where you get the full experience!

While enjoying a pint in a small European city this past summer, I inserted myself into a conversation between a bartender and one of his regulars. As we see in many of our US cities, parking has become more and more difficult in downtowns. The solution? The local government raised the parking rates to $35 for each three-hour block of time. The assumption that the city councilors made was that this would ease congestion and, although the citizens would be annoyed, they would soon adjust and either pay the higher amount or start taking public transportation.

But, in fact, just the opposite happened, because what the city government failed to do was also raise the fine for violating the parking ordinance. When enforced, someone who fails to pay for parking gets a $35 fine. The local law stated that you can only be cited for the same violation twice in one day. You guessed it, the breakeven was now six hours. If you intended to park for six hours or more, your best bet was NOT to pay for parking, hoping you wouldn't get a ticket, but knowing that even if you did you may still come out ahead. The government was playing checkers, but their residents were playing chess!

This had me reflect on a presentation I saw at an industry conference two years ago. I had the opportunity to hear the deputy director of the Employee Benefits Security Administration (EBSA) speak. The presentation was interactive, and the conversation centered around the decision to mandate automatic enrollment on January 1, 2025, for 401(k) plans that began after December 29, 2022, with more than ten employees. We were all 401(k) specialists in the room, so there was no debate on the merits of this decision, as we all knew that this would increase participation.

So, naturally, we assumed that since auto-enroll was going to be mandated, the SECURE Act 2.0 $500 tax credit for companies with fewer than one hundred employees "choosing" to put an auto-enroll provision in their plan document would be rescinded. Of course, I wouldn't be writing about this if that were the case! Those two decisions were mutually exclusive, and the IRS would now pay plan sponsors $1,500 over a three-year period to do something the Department of Labor was *requiring* them to do!

In the end, none of these moments—the tiny Swedish pour, the crowded craps table, or the downtown parking gamble—were financially devastating on their own. But they all reveal the same truth: Small numbers, misunderstood assumptions, and hidden incentives can quietly work against us when we're not paying attention. Whether you're ordering a drink, placing a bet, or making decisions that will shape your financial future, the math is always there in the background. You don't have to calculate everything yourself, but you do want someone in your corner who understands how the numbers really work. Because, in the long run, clarity compounds just as powerfully as confusion.

Last year on the day after Thanksgiving, I hung two sets of indoor holiday lights. One took me three minutes; the other took thirty. The difference? Last year I carefully wrapped one string of lights around a rectangular piece of Styrofoam I've been using for years. The other set—those blinking LEDs—had been hastily shoved away in a completely illogical ball of confusion.

For the past five years, whenever I opened the holiday storage bins, I chose the neatly wrapped set and conveniently ignored the tangled mess I had created. But with a little extra time on my hands that day, I decided to face the "bundle of joy" and see whether it was even salvageable. It was, but not without far more effort than it deserved.

That small win got me thinking about the many things in life that seem simple when we put them away but become a much bigger project if we ignore them for too long. If you've read anything I've written, you know I'm a big believer in auto-enroll and auto-increase features in company-sponsored retirement plans. Yet there's another feature recordkeepers offer that many participants overlook: auto-rebalance.

Deciding between taking an aggressive approach to investing versus being conservative is very much a personal choice. When meeting with clients, they'll often ask me my opinion on how much risk to take. Although it sounds evasive, I tell them the truth is that they know their risk profile better than anyone. If I know the right questions to identify the appropriate risk, they just need to answer them honestly.

But what if a client thinks they're taking the safe route, and it turns out the passage of time inadvertently makes their portfolio too risky? This is where automatic rebalancing strategies can make a big difference.

In taxable brokerage accounts, selling investments can trigger taxable gains or losses. That's not the case in qualified retirement plans. They're intentionally designed so that rebalancing—selling the investments that have grown faster and adding to those that lagged—does not create a taxable event. Auto-rebalance resets your allocation to the percentages you originally intended, keeping your strategy aligned with your goals.

Take a simple example. If your target was 70 percent stocks and 30 percent bonds and you never touched your account for thirty years, historical averages suggest your portfolio would drift to roughly 91 percent stocks and 9 percent bonds. That creates two issues:

- First, you may have taken a "set it and forget it" approach and have no idea how far your allocation has drifted.

- Second, as we approach retirement, we tend to get more conservative, not more aggressive.

Target-date funds and managed accounts can reduce or eliminate this problem. But if you prefer to choose your own investments in your 401(k), enabling auto-rebalance may be an equally effective solution.

So, as you open your 401(k) "storage bin" this holiday season, take a moment to see whether your recordkeeper offers auto-rebalance. It could prevent an unnecessary tangle later on and help keep your retirement strategy on track.

CHAPTER 8

RULES, LOOPHOLES, AND THE SPACE BETWEEN

always thought it was a term of endearment when my mother called me a late bloomer academically. I suppose I focused on the *bloomer* part more than the *late*, but the more I think about it, the less convinced I am that it was meant as a compliment. In high school, grades of B and B+ felt perfectly acceptable. Getting a C on the report card usually came with restrictions in the fun department, while achieving an A set my parents' expectations uncomfortably high.

My friend Peter, on the other hand, would do just about anything for an A, and that included cheating on tests. Cheating, of course, is an obvious character flaw and not really up for debate. But even setting that aside, I was amazed by the lengths he was willing to go to gain an advantage.

It has been a long time since I was in school, and I imagine exams today are far more structured and tightly proctored. Back then, it was much simpler: Answer the questions on paper and hand the test in when you are done.

Teachers were particularly good at spotting wandering eyes, and the smart students were even better at protecting their answers. In the days leading up to a test, Peter and I would get together to "study" at his house. In reality, those sessions quickly turned into Van Halen and Pink Floyd listening parties. With one day left and fully aware that I hadn't put in the work, I crammed the night before, just enough to maintain my preferred strategy of flying under the radar.

Peter took quite a different approach. He spent hours preparing what had to be the world's smallest cheat sheet, one that fit neatly into the palm of his hand. Writing in a font so small it still doesn't exist in Microsoft Word, he meticulously combed through each chapter of the textbook, pulling out anything he thought might appear on the test and writing it down. When he finished, he laminated the tiny index card with clear tape to prevent smudging, fully aware there was a good chance he'd be sweating while trying to avoid detection.

I lost touch with Peter after high school, but I have to assume his methods continued into college and probably became even more sophisticated. Let's just hope he didn't become a doctor.

Early in my career as a financial advisor, my firm financially incentivized me to enroll in a two-year program to earn a professional certification in financial planning. The coursework required to sit for the CERTIFIED FINANCIAL PLANNER™ exam was extensive. Still, I knew there was a reward if I passed, and more importantly, I knew it would make me a better advisor for my clients.

The exam was administered over two days, back when it was still paper based, before the transition to computerized testing in 2014. I arrived on the first day with a bottle of water, which was promptly confiscated. The proctor explained that only two pencils and scrap paper were allowed. No big deal, I thought, although I couldn't quite understand why a sealed bottle of water was considered a threat.

As I was leaving the testing site that afternoon, curiosity got the best of me and I asked. The proctor explained that candidates had previously been caught writing answers on the inside of clear plastic water bottle labels. They would carefully steam off the label, write notes on the inside, and then reattach it as if nothing had happened. Peter, upgraded.

I found this insane. Once again, I couldn't help thinking that the time spent creating these elaborate aids would have been far better spent actually studying. The proctor went on to tell me that water bottles weren't the only casualty. Candy had also been banned. Cheaters had devised intricate coding systems using M&M's and Skittles: The number of candies indicated the question, and the color revealed the multiple-choice answer. Ingenious, I suppose, but exhausting.

What always struck me, both then and now, is that the effort required to cheat often exceeds the effort required to prepare. Whether it was Peter's microscopic handwriting or the engineering feat of a reattached water bottle label, the common thread was misplaced energy.

Looking back, maybe being a "late bloomer" wasn't about intelligence at all. It was about learning slowly, that shortcuts rarely save time in the long run. The real advantage doesn't come from clever work-arounds or hidden notes. It comes from doing unglamorous work when no one is watching, even if the results don't immediately stand out on a report card or a test score.

What if you aren't cheating, but instead taking advantage of the way the rules are written, even if it wasn't how they were intended? And is that the same thing as a loophole?

The Philadelphia Eagles began implementing the now-infamous "tush push" during the 2022 season, and it quickly became one of the most reliable short-yardage plays in football. The simplest way to describe it is this: It's a quarterback sneak where the quarterback takes the snap and immediately drives forward, while large teammates behind him physically push everyone across the line to gain yards. When executed properly, the defense knows exactly what's coming and still finds it nearly impossible to stop.

Many teams cried foul. Others added it to their own playbooks. Yet no one has executed it with the same consistency as the Eagles. What hasn't happened, at least as of this writing, is the play being outlawed by the NFL, which the league could easily do during any offseason rules committee meeting. The rules allow it. The Eagles simply execute it better than everyone else.

This isn't a new phenomenon.

In 1951, Bill Veeck, then owner of the St. Louis Browns, signed 3-foot-7-inch Eddie Gaedel to a Major League Baseball contract. The strike zone in baseball is defined as the area between a batter's shoulders and knees. Logic would suggest that the smaller the batter, the smaller the strike zone, and the harder it becomes for a pitcher to throw a strike. In Gaedel's only plate appearance, he was instructed not to swing. He walked on four straight pitches and was immediately replaced by a pinch runner.

Major League Baseball responded swiftly, voiding Gaedel's contract shortly thereafter to ensure no one tried the same stunt again. Gaedel didn't cheat. He didn't break a rule. He exposed an assumption that the rules quietly relied on.

A more recent example has emerged in youth baseball, including games leading up to the Little League World Series. Normally, runners work hard to avoid getting caught in a rundown situation where they're stranded between bases and almost certain to be tagged out. At the professional level, teams devote significant practice time to executing rundowns properly. Youth teams do not.

Some aggressive coaches began instructing hitters, after reaching first base safely, to intentionally drift toward second and force a rundown if a teammate was on or approaching third. While the defense focuses on the runner caught between bases, attention shifts away from home plate, allowing the runner on third to score. The batter-runner is often eventually called out, but trading an out for a run is almost always a favorable exchange.

There's no rule preventing this. The objections tend to focus on sportsmanship, not legality. And just like the tush push, nothing prevents opposing teams from doing the same thing, if they choose to.

If cheating is easy to define, and we've now seen multiple examples of people taking advantage of rules that weren't intended to work a certain way, how is this different from a loophole?

A loophole is something else entirely. A loophole exists when a benefit arises not from skillful execution, but from a structural gap, when separate provisions were never meant to interact the way they do. The outcome isn't just unexpected; it's misaligned with the purpose of the rule itself.

Sometimes things can't be defined as either cheating or loopholes. Rule exploitation presents plenty of examples in the US tax code. One example seen often in my line of work is the Mega Backdoor Roth conversion. This strategy allows high-income earners, who would otherwise be ineligible for Roth contributions, to move tens of thousands of dollars per year into Roth accounts. By permitting after-tax contributions inside a 401(k) plan and allowing those dollars to be converted to Roth, the tax code unintentionally created a pathway that lawmakers never explicitly designed.

To be clear, this is not cheating. But it isn't simply mastery of the rules either.

While writing this, I was reminded of something I used to tell my sales teams when they asked about tactical decisions: *As long as it's legal, moral, and ethical, go for it.* Cheating fails that test immediately. Loopholes pass the legal test, but may fail the moral or ethical one, depending on perspective. Rule exploitation lives somewhere in between, where the rules are followed precisely, even if the outcome makes people uncomfortable.

And maybe that's the real takeaway. The question isn't whether an advantage exists. It's whether you can defend how you got it, without hiding it, justifying it, or hoping no one looks too closely.

COMPOUNDING: IT'S NOT JUST FOR FINANCE ANYMORE

O n December 1, 1991, I rented a U-Haul for $500 to move 344 miles from Stamford, Connecticut, to Rochester, New York. What I didn't realize was that the "cost" of that twenty-four-foot box truck wasn't really $500; it was nearly $138,000.

You've probably seen similar examples when reading about compounding interest: stories meant to shock, teach patience, and highlight the magic of money earning money. Mine isn't hypothetical, though. It's a very real reminder of how one financial decision can echo for decades.

After nearly two years in my entry-level job, I was offered the opportunity to move to corporate headquarters for a job in the Information Systems Department. This promotion came with a significant pay increase, as my salary would increase from $20,800 per year to $22,000 annually, with an opportunity for another bump in pay after six months. What it didn't include was a relocation package, which didn't seem to matter to me since I could now move out of a shared apartment with two roommates to my very own 440-square-foot basement studio apartment.

The only problem was that I didn't have the money for the move. Luckily, I had been participating in the company stock purchase plan, and my account had a value of just over $500. My father offered to lend me the money so I didn't need to cash in the stock, but I was too proud and turned down his offer. The company stock was trading at a split-adjusted price of 51 cents a share at the time. Fast-forward to 2025 when the stock hit $140, and that little $500 account would have been worth nearly $138,000.

That decision taught me two lessons I still carry into my work today. First, compounding can turn small amounts into life-changing sums if you give it time. Second, short-term needs can undermine long-term growth if you don't have liquid savings to fall back on.

In my work as a 401(k) specialist, I often encourage plan participants to contribute as much as they can afford into the company retirement plan. Certainly, maximize the company match, I say, but also stretch yourself a little if you can and increase your deferrals even more. Our team suggests employees consider adding auto escalation so that their contributions are increased each year by a percentage point or two. We believe strongly in this, and not much will change our minds. No one has ever gotten to their retirement party with "too much money." However, it's also important to have an emergency savings account for surprises so that you're not forced to dip into those retirement accounts when something unexpected happens.

Fortunately, most 401(k) plans allow for access to your funds before you turn 59 ½ years old, the age where you can start drawing down your balance without penalties. The most common way to access your funds is through a loan, which is actually borrowing money from yourself. The interest goes back into your 401(k) account as well, so, on the surface, this seems like a very reasonable way to "bridge" an unexpected expense. But there's a catch. If you leave your job, that loan becomes due in most cases. If you can't afford to pay it back, then the balance in your plan is often used to pay back the loan—and just like that, your retirement savings account is significantly depleted.

So, while building your retirement savings, also make sure you have at least three months of living expenses set aside in a high-yield savings account. That cushion can prevent you from needing a loan, or worse, cashing out retirement funds, when life throws you a curveball. And if you're fortunate enough to have a generous relative offering a helping hand, think carefully before turning it down. Pride can be expensive, but it doesn't have to cost you $138,000.

We talk about *compounding* every day when it comes to investments, but compounding occurs in all facets of life. The irrational fear that something unused for ten years might suddenly prove useful tomorrow fuels the hoarding instinct we all try to avoid.

I have a client who builds self-storage facilities, and they tell me they've never been busier. I believe it. My family recently moved into a new community, and two years in, most of our neighbors have now relocated their cars from the garage, permanently parking them in their driveways. How does everyone accumulate so much stuff?

In business, we often borrow from the Eisenhower Matrix—the "three D's": *Do it, Delegate it, or Discard it.* Personally, I've learned that "Discard it" deserves the most attention. And I wouldn't exactly call myself a minimalist.

For most of my career, I've managed teams, often stepping into roles vacated by leaders who had been promoted or moved on. One book that consistently guided my early decision-making was *The First 90 Days* by Michael Watkins. It asks whether your assignment is a start-up, a turnaround, a realignment, or a sustainment of success.

In one assignment, on the first day of what I'd classify as a turnaround project, my new assistant, who had stayed on from the previous manager, scheduled time with me to review *"all the reports"* I would need. I had never seen anything like it. She forwarded, printed, and collated volumes of spreadsheets analyzing every conceivable metric of my sales teams and their managers. She was remarkably intelligent and could tell me exactly where each number came from, whether she extracted it from our CRM or rolled it up from the various districts that reported to me.

By Thursday afternoon, she would assemble a towering stack of reports so that I could spend all day Friday reviewing them. That was not my idea of a productive Friday. The manager I replaced wasn't around to explain what to do with these reports, and while I understood how the input was collected, I had no idea what value the output provided.

As it turned out, most of the data wasn't useful. Over the years, every new initiative, product, or team goal had generated its own custom report, but none were ever discarded.

I remember that first day vividly. It became a permanent reminder that accumulation, whether in garages or organizations, happens quietly, one item or report at a time.

As our advisory team continues to grow, we remind ourselves of the three D's, especially the last one. If we add a report or a custom field in our CRM, we commit to eliminating two.

The same principle applies to our lives and our garages: If we want room to grow, we have to make room to breathe.

Oh, and my wife and I still fit both cars in the garage. *For now.*

Whether we identify as a hoarder, or fit nicely into the minimalist camp, I think we all could agree that obsessing over either is unhealthy.

In the summer of 2025, it was announced that the family of Jerry Buss sold the Los Angeles Lakers NBA team for a record $10 billion! What was even more amazing was that Mr. Buss purchased the team in 1979 for "just" $67.5 million. Then I read somewhere else that the return on the investment for this franchise was actually LOWER than the compounded annualized return of the S&P 500 index during this same time period.

Now, an investment-centric numbers geek would find this very interesting and probably start digging in even deeper on this factoid. But they would completely miss the point. What they wouldn't and can't calculate is "return on enjoyment." The Buss family sat either courtside or in the owner's luxury box for forty-six seasons and a total of eleven championships! What value would you place on that?

The forty-six years of the Buss family Lakers ownership is identical to the length of someone's career if they start working at twenty-one years old and retire at sixty-seven years old. During enrollment meetings for 401(k) plans, and most interactions between financial advisors and their clients, a disproportionate amount of attention and time is spent discussing stocks and bonds and many other asset classes. They'll talk about compounding and risk-adjusted returns, alpha, beta, and probably a few other Greek letters. They'll emphasize the importance of diversification and asset allocation, and, yes—this is all very important! But … is it interesting? I'm in the business, and I promise you, it's not.

So, what is interesting to the average 401(k) plan participant or retail investor? Not the dollars themselves, but instead what they get to do with that money! And that's where "return on enjoyment" comes in. Will a larger balance in their 401(k) account when they retire allow them to travel more? Spend time with family and friends? Finally buy the '67 Corvette that made no sense when they were working? To maximize the value of our interactions with prospective clients or existing accounts, we don't focus on the dollars and cents, but instead the tangible rewards that nest egg provides. In other words, ensuring that they prepare themselves for more memories and life experiences, much like the Buss family was able to accomplish with the Lakers.

Well, if this inspires you to buy a professional sports franchise, then start saving up now! If the NBA seems out of reach, you may be happy to know that buying a minor league hockey team is a little more reasonable, as the Allen Americans in Texas recently sold for what's believed to be about $2.5 million. That's the good news. The bad news is that they finished last in their division this past year with only sixteen wins in seventy-two games!

CHAPTER 10

BEYOND THE BALANCE SHEET: THE REAL VALUE OF GOODWILL

No business ever wants to lose clients. When it happens, good leaders typically conduct some form of an After-Action Review (AAR) to understand what went wrong and how to prevent it from happening again. At its best, an AAR is not about assigning blame; it's about organizational learning and process improvement.

But what if client attrition isn't the result of a specific failure at all? What if it's simply the consequence of operating in an industry that is slowly becoming obsolete?

We've seen this before. Landline home telephones were once a staple in every household. They didn't disappear overnight, but their relevance eroded as technology changed. That example is obvious in hindsight. More subtle are industries where the core product can survive, but only if the go-to-market strategy evolves, sometimes dramatically.

Netflix and Blockbuster provide one of the clearest contrasts in adaptability. If you're a millennial or younger, you likely know Netflix only as a streaming giant, as common in today's homes as a phone line was in 1970. What's often forgotten is that Netflix began as a mail-based DVD rental service. When it was launched in 1997, its subscription model, unlimited rentals for a flat monthly fee, was already a departure from industry norms.

More importantly, Netflix leadership anticipated the decline of physical media almost from the start. Long before DVDs peaked, they were planning for a broadband-enabled future. The result is the platform that now lives on nearly every screen we own.

Blockbuster, on the other hand, was always playing defense. Faced with a true disrupter, its leadership was never fully committed to change. Their response mimicked Netflix's original model, mail-out rentals, but still required in-store returns. When Netflix went digital, Blockbuster hedged again, treating streaming as an experiment rather than a foundational shift in the business.

At its peak, Blockbuster operated more than 9,000 stores and employed roughly 84,000 people worldwide. By 2010, the company was bankrupt. Its last store closed in 2014.

That raises a broader question: Which industries are being challenged by digital disrupters today, and how are they responding?

It would be easy for me to focus on 401(k) recordkeepers, an industry I work closely with every day, but that hits a little too close to home. A more neutral example might be home security systems and alarm monitoring.

I had been a client of a legacy alarm company for eleven years. Over that time, response times worsened, technical errors on an aging control panel became routine, and costs steadily increased, without meaningful service improvements or product upgrades. Meanwhile, newer entrants were offering modern technology, smart-home integrations, flexible monitoring options, and no long-term contracts.

Eventually, the value being offered by the new service was too compelling to stay with the old firm.

Before canceling my existing service, I purchased hardware from one of these newer providers, reassured by a solid return policy. I wanted to confirm that the self-installation experience was truly as simple as advertised before ripping outdated sensors off every wall and door in my house. It was. Setup was straightforward, intuitive, and exactly as promised.

Canceling the old service, however, was anything but.

I logged into the legacy provider's outdated web portal and searched every profile and account setting for a cancellation option. After several minutes of coming up empty, I opened the chat window, decidedly not AI-powered, and asked how to cancel. The response was blunt: Cancellation could only be handled by calling a toll-free number. Because it was after business hours, I was told to call back when they reopened. This struck me as odd for an alarm monitoring company. Shouldn't they always be open?

During business hours the next day, I mentally prepared for what I assumed would be a frustrating call. After navigating a maze of phone prompts to reach the cancellation department, I was placed on hold. The prerecorded message suggested that, instead of waiting, I should visit their website. Was this outdated technology, or a deliberate attempt to get me to hang up and lose my place in the queue, knowing full well that cancellation couldn't be done online? I gave them the benefit of the doubt, but it didn't inspire confidence.

As expected, I was routed to a retention specialist. I reminded myself that the person on the other end of the phone was simply doing their job. Frustration directed at them would be misplaced.

Retention teams, after all, are just sales teams by another name. Their compensation is often tied directly to keeping clients from leaving. I was polite but firm. I made it clear I wasn't going to be persuaded.

The offers came quickly: 30 percent off if I committed to another five-year contract. Then 50 percent off with no contract at all. At one point, I couldn't help but ask why none of these options had been presented before I decided to cancel.

Finally, as my patience wore thin, I asked if we could simply complete the process. That's when I heard something truly astonishing.

"I can't," she said. "My company requires me to keep you on the phone for ten minutes or more before I'm allowed to hit the CANCEL button."

We agreed she would put me on hold while we both checked our emails until the clock ran out. Exactly ten minutes later, she returned, processed the cancellation, and the call ended.

The takeaway? Losing a client is not always a failure of service or execution. Sometimes it's the result of refusing to acknowledge that the world has changed. Blockbuster didn't fail because it lacked customers; it failed because it clung to a business model long after its relevance faded. The same pattern plays out whenever companies invest more energy in retention tactics than in reinvention.

When friction becomes a strategy and inconvenience is mistaken for loyalty, clients don't stay, they just leave later, and with far less goodwill. The real lesson isn't about how hard it should be to cancel. It's about how easy it should be to stay.

On more than one occasion, I've spoken to two business owners in the exact same industry, one saying business is so busy they can't come up for air, the other insisting times look bleak. How is that possible, and who's right?

Why are there sixty-minute wait times at some restaurants, while on the same evening, in the same town, you can walk straight into others? The obvious answer is better food or service, but I think it runs deeper than that. We talk about compounding all the time in the investment world yet rarely apply it to decision-making. Good decisions and bad ones quietly add to or subtract from the goodwill bank, and when customers stop seeing a balance, that's when they vote with their feet.

My favorite restaurant is less than two miles from my house. The food is good, not great, and they've made their share of mistakes over the years we've been going there. Still, my wife and I faithfully return every Thursday for Martini Night. More than just knowing the bartenders' names, and them knowing ours, we actually know each other. They know about our vacations, and we know when they've gotten engaged or are expecting a child. Turnover among the staff is incredibly low, so much so that general managers come and go more frequently than the servers.

A few years ago, one of the newer managers came up with a great idea (cue the sarcasm): a loyalty program. For $25 a year, customers would get discounts, invitations to special events, and a free dessert on their birthday. The logic was that the value far exceeded the cost. What that manager failed to realize was that our loyalty wasn't to a plastic card or a sign out front; it was to the bartenders and servers. We joined anyway, mostly because one of them could win a contest for signing up the most customers.

In what might be the shortest loyalty program in restaurant history, the "exclusive" club was canceled just two months later. Of course they'd refund our membership fee, right? Nope. The new manager pointed to fine print saying the program could be canceled at any time. Knowing this person was likely a short-timer, we shared the story with one of the bartenders, not looking for anything in return, just quietly signaling that this manager might not fit the culture of our neighborhood watering hole.

And, entirely by coincidence, a couple of our martinis vanished from the next check. Also, by coincidence, our tip that night grew by roughly the same amount. What could have been a serious withdrawal from the goodwill bank turned into a few meaningful deposits, made by the staff, not management.

Another management decision I've noticed popping up lately is passing credit card processing fees directly to customers. If margins are tight, I guess that makes sense. But I've seen this at restaurants where the average check is $50 a head. Would you notice if the French dip was $18 instead of $18.75, and would that change your decision? The price difference wouldn't register for me. I have no idea what it costs to make a prime rib sandwich, so it wouldn't influence what I ordered. But I absolutely notice a new line item at the bottom of the check adding 3.5 percent for using a credit card.

Just because you can do something doesn't mean you should. We recently stopped going to a veterinary clinic because they charged me $10 to reprint our dog's heartworm prescription—not for the medication itself, but for the ink and paper.

The businesses that thrive aren't always the ones with the best products, lowest prices, or cleverest policies. They're the ones that understand goodwill compounds, slowly, quietly, and relentlessly, just like money does. Every small decision is either a deposit or a withdrawal. Over time, those balances determine whether customers make reservations, walk-ins, or simply walk away. The lesson is simple: Optimize for trust, not transactions. The returns are far greater.

I had a business owner ask me recently if he could legally discriminate in his 401(k) plan by offering different matches for different classes of employees. I'm glad he asked me instead of ChatGPT, and I didn't immediately make any assumptions just by the way the question was phrased. Instead, I responded with a number of clarifying questions to understand his goals for the plan.

Clients will often give you the solution and ask for validation versus taking a more curious approach. Through a series of questions, I was able to identify his objectives (no, it wasn't to hurt his lower-paid employees) and offer some ideas that didn't involve paying a third-party administrator (TPA) thousands of dollars a year to write a custom document. His current prototype adoption agreement was just fine as it was.

For kicks and giggles, I figured I'd ask ChatGPT the exact same question and see how they'd answer it. You guessed it—they outlined the precise step-by-step process for how to offer different matches to different employees. How to change the plan document, how to hire a TPA, and the entire playbook for what would end up being a terrible idea (and very expensive to reverse when the client realizes it).

The difference between humans and machines? For starters, AI answers it literally as "can I do it?" and an empathetic human takes the approach of "should I do it?"

That's not to say that there aren't an amazing number of applications that leverage the rapid advancement of artificial intelligence. The incredibly cool, choreographed drone show that I went to last year to celebrate Independence Day in our small little town would never have happened a few years back.

In the end, my client didn't really have a compliance question; he had a leadership decision to make. Sure, we could have rewritten the plan and jumped through the regulatory hoops. But every time an employer tweaks benefits to save a few dollars, employees notice. And they remember.

That's the part no algorithm measures very well. Goodwill isn't just something you build with customers at the point of sale; it's something you either build or erode every time you make a decision that affects your team.

AI can tell you what's possible. Good advisors, and good leaders, help you think through what's wise. And when it comes to long-term business health, goodwill with your employees is almost always money well spent.

Unlike many who venture into sales as a career, I never found prospecting for new business particularly challenging. In fact, I enjoyed it. Meeting new people, especially business owners, often meant hearing personal stories that were both interesting and inspirational. And perhaps there was a screw loose somewhere, because I never had much of a fear of rejection either.

Where I struggled early on was price negotiation. I believed so strongly in the value of what I was offering that I felt it should never be discounted. That sounds noble in theory, but it wasn't how things worked in New York. Not even close. Haggling wasn't optional; it was practically a sport.

As a rookie sales rep, we were allowed to discount our services by up to 15 percent and lock that price in for one year. With manager approval, you could extend it to two years, and with a director's sign-off, up to three.

My biggest competitor took a very different approach. Whenever I lost a sale, I made a habit of asking what I could have done differently. Occasionally, that question reopened the door and turned a loss into a win. More often, it simply offered a lesson for the next opportunity. Over time, I kept hearing the same refrain: The competitor was offering a "discount valid for life."

Eventually, I learned how to handle that objection with two simple questions. First, did you ask the competitor's sales rep how long they planned to work there? And second, did they expect to work there for their entire life so they could personally ensure that the discount was honored for that duration?

It was delivered sarcastically—you can get away with that in the Northeast—but it usually made the point. The prospective client would pause and realize that this was less a promise and more a sales tactic, one that likely wouldn't stand the test of time.

Years later, I watched a similar lesson play out in a very different setting. A private golf club, facing financial strain, offered members the option to convert their annual dues into a "lifetime" membership in exchange for a large, onetime payment. On paper, the math could be made to work, especially when stretched across decades and adjusted for inflation. A meaningful number of members accepted the offer, providing the club with much-needed cash.

Not long afterward, the club was sold. The new ownership group had purchased the assets, not the liabilities, and took the position that the lifetime memberships were obligations of the prior owners. As a result, those agreements were no longer honored as originally promised.

A similar issue has surfaced in the world of college athletics. Long-time season ticket holders at a major university were informed that stadium renovations would eliminate their seats, effectively ending "lifetime" agreements signed decades earlier for prime locations. Changing circumstances had rendered the original promises impractical, if not impossible, to maintain.

In both cases, negotiations followed. Settlements were discussed. Compromises were reached. And while no one walked away thrilled, reality eventually replaced expectation.

The easy takeaway is "if it sounds too good to be true," but we've all heard that before. A more useful question, when presented with any "lifetime" offer, is simply: Why are they offering this? And just as importantly, what is the true breakeven point if the promise is eventually reinterpreted, or not honored at all?

And if I had more time on my hands, it might be interesting to revisit some of those sales I lost decades ago and see whether that lifetime discount my competitor once offered is still being applied.

* * *

The word *value* appears multiple times in this book, and I think intuitively we all understand when something has value, or, more importantly, when we perceive value. Simply stated, value is the surplus created when what you receive exceeds what you pay.

Academically, an economist might say that value can be calculated as benefits minus price. The larger the difference, the greater the value. Negative results may indicate a lack of perceived value.

Reflecting on the Buss family's forty-six years of ownership of the Los Angeles Lakers, I'm certain most would agree that the benefits exceeded the price.

But is there such a thing as too much value? And what if the cost is zero—how does that affect the formula?

I recently attended a Small Business Expo after multiple solicitations landed in my inbox. The price was "free," and with plenty of hyperbole, the organizers promoted the event as the best networking experience ever. The convention center was only about forty minutes from my house, so the real cost was simply the time I committed to the event.

The organizers advertised that the expo floor would open at exactly 9:30 a.m., yet we were held in the foyer until ten. A huge banner hung over the entrance that read, ANYONE CAUGHT SOLICITING BUSINESS AT THE BOOTHS WILL BE REMOVED IMMEDIATELY.

Now I have been in and around sales for my entire professional career, and I still can't quite figure out how, in a business environment, you "network" with someone without telling them what you do for a living and what a good client looks like for you. According to the rules, that would qualify for immediate expulsion. Needless to say, my time at the convention was short, and my perceived value received was negative.

What about too much value?

Since this is the first book I've written, I needed to outsource quite a few tasks to get it published. I was squarely in the "I don't know what I don't know" camp, so I did quite a bit of research to determine that I needed a copy editor, a line editor, a cover artist, a typesetter, and a proofreader. Through multiple conversations, I was able to get a fairly tight range of what each of these services would cost.

Now I simply needed to meet with the finalists in each category and determine where I believed I would get the most value. Much to my surprise, one of the websites I researched must have used cookies to identify me, because right before I finalized my team they offered me a "limited-time 65% discount" on every service I needed.

Sounds great, right?

I passed.

I assumed there must be something missing. I was getting close to my self-imposed deadlines, and there was too much risk involved if what they were offering turned out to be a slimmed-down version of what I actually needed.

The simple formula of benefits minus price works well on paper, but in real life the equation is more nuanced. Free events can waste your time, and deep discounts can introduce uncertainty rather than savings. True value isn't determined by price alone; it comes from confidence that what you're receiving will actually deliver the benefit you expect.

CHAPTER 11

THE POWER OF THE INTENTIONAL PAUSE

There are a few business principles I tend to repeat often, probably in direct proportion to how tired my partners are of hearing them. One of my favorites is, "*If we can't scale it, I don't want to do it.*"

While not a perfect antonym, the opposite of scale is inefficiency. Which raises an interesting question: Are there such things as *intentional* inefficiencies?

I'm confident the answer is yes, because I practice a few of them myself. Chief among them is my absolute refusal to use mail merge for emails or marketing campaigns. In my experience, the only thing guaranteed about mail merge is that something will go wrong, and when it does, it will happen on a very large scale. Instead, I use the clipboard tools built into Microsoft applications and still compose messages one at a time. It's slower, but it's far easier to catch a mistake before it's too late.

Holidays provide a much-needed pause and an ideal opportunity to embrace intentional inefficiency. Handwriting Christmas cards. Hanging lights. Making phone calls (remember those?) to people you haven't spoken to in a while. (No, following someone on Facebook or LinkedIn does not count.) Because of this, I commit to not using the word *scale* for at least a couple of weeks at the end of December each year.

And while I'm generally a fan of outsourcing mundane tasks, especially when the cost is lower than the value I place on my time, there are some things that either can't or shouldn't be delegated. One example I find particularly amusing is the growing business of hiring professionals to hang exterior holiday lights. Our neighborhood streets are unusually narrow, so when work trucks line both sides, navigating through them requires both patience and precision. Every November and December, I have to carefully drive around workers hauling ladders and boxes of lights to homes where decorations are being installed professionally.

To be fair, since all of my decorations are indoors, and I avoid ladders whenever possible, I can't judge anyone for outsourcing that task. But I do draw the line at something I read about a few years ago. A father in New Jersey proudly told a reporter that he hired someone to trim his family's Christmas tree. I couldn't help but wonder whether Bing Crosby and Brenda Lee would need to rewrite their holiday classics if outsourced tree trimming had actually caught on.

Thankfully, that's the last time I've heard of a stranger entering someone's home to place personal ornaments on the tree.

Our country lost a true sports pioneer in February of 2026, and although you may not know his name, you are certainly familiar with his legacy. In the early 1970s, Jeff Galloway was considered one of the most talented distance runners in the United States, making the Olympic team in 1972 and setting the American ten-mile road record the following year. Yet his greatest contributions to the sport came after he retired from competitive running.

Galloway opened Phidippides, a specialty running store in the Buckhead section of Atlanta, at a time when specialty running retail was still a niche experiment. Most shoes and athletic apparel were sold in general sporting goods stores. But it was what Jeff gave away for free—his advice—that made his store, and later his chain, the community hub for recreational runners.

Many might say Galloway simply benefited from the running boom of that era. I would argue the opposite: He was less a beneficiary and more of a driving force. Galloway helped democratize running by emphasizing finishing over winning. While coaching and developing recreational runners, he created "The Galloway Method," which encouraged athletes to alternate running with planned walk breaks. Purists viewed this as inefficient. But by lowering the barrier to entry, he invited thousands, perhaps millions, of people who might never have laced up their shoes to begin a lifelong pursuit of fitness and health.

Although I was a high school cross-country runner, my own fifteen-year hiatus from the sport ended when my tailor politely informed me there was no fabric left to let out my suits. It was in a middle school auditorium in Orlando where I first saw Jeff speak, and his explicit permission to ease back into running was all I needed to get started. I think it's safe to say I would not have joined the YMCA running group, where I met my wife, without the gentle nudge Jeff provided that evening.

It's a neurological fact that exercise, especially aerobic exercise, increases brain activity. So, it's no surprise that many of my best writing ideas are hatched while jogging around our neighborhood. Since it would look a little strange to carry a notepad and pen with me, I head straight to my home office when I return and write down my thoughts before they disappear. On a typical Friday morning before work, I would normally run three miles straight through, no walk breaks, eyes on the clock. This time was different. I decided to honor Jeff Galloway's legacy by deliberately taking walk breaks throughout the run while reflecting on his contributions to the running community.

And somewhere between those intentional pauses, the larger lesson came into focus. What looks inefficient at the moment often proves transformational over time. Galloway's walk breaks did not make running weaker; they made it accessible. They did not slow the sport down; they expanded it. In business and in life, we are often conditioned to eliminate friction, compress timelines, and optimize every step. But sometimes the smarter move is the one that appears slower on paper. Intentional inefficiency, when applied thoughtfully, isn't wasted motion; it's strategic inclusion. Jeff Galloway understood that long before most of us were paying attention.

I tried to retire in July of 2021, and it lasted exactly thirty-eight days. It seems kind of strange that I now spend most of each day showing 401(k) plan participants how to save and invest their money to prepare for a fulfilling and dignified retirement! No, I didn't run out of money in the first month like my tennis friends like to joke about. However, I wasn't prepared for the immediate lack of purpose I felt.

My experience isn't unique. In fact, what I've come to see is a broader shift in how retirement is defined across generations. What I have learned since then is that retirement can be defined in many ways. Not only does retirement look different for everyone, but it also makes a big difference if you're retiring to something versus retiring from something.

Anyone who's from the Gen X or millennial generation likely witnessed parents and grandparents working for one or two companies their entire career, receiving a pension, and then spending their golden years traveling, visiting family, and playing way too many rounds of golf.

Things have changed dramatically. The "hard stop" seems more the exception than the rule these days. Yes, there are still communities like The Villages in Florida where every moment of the day can be filled with pickleball, card games, and happy hour, but I'm seeing more examples of people taking on second careers because they want to work as opposed to need to work.

The best example I've seen of this in a long time was when I had a free Sunday afternoon last summer and decided to drive an hour to Spartanburg, South Carolina, for the Hub City Spartanburgers minor league baseball game. As many clubs will do, they had a special event that day celebrating the long history of baseball in the Upstate. Throwing out the first pitch was Archie Means, who from 1958 to 1960 was the second baseman for the Spartanburg Sluggers, a semiprofessional team that drew big crowds—over sixty-five years ago!

While looking for a hot dog and a beer in the concourse, I noticed a couple of folding tables set up in the shaded area. Two gentlemen were there signing autographs—Archie himself and another man who also looked to be in his eighties or beyond. Since the line was short, I was able to have a nice chat with both of them. Prepared to talk about baseball, instead I found myself in a lengthy discussion with Archie about his barbershop on East Kennedy Street, just two city blocks away, where he'd been cutting hair for over fifty years! Mr. Means was proud of the fact that he still works four hours a day—he showed no signs of slowing, and the joy on his face told me he is making the most of his retirement!

The other gentleman was Edwin Epps, the author of *Duncan Park: Stories of a Classic American Ballpark*. Mr. Epps was a schoolteacher for forty years, and then immediately pivoted to a second career as a writer. We talked about his books, his freelance journalism work, and even poetry! He was proud of his career as an educator, but equally passionate about his second act of town historian and published author.

So, you don't have to retire and immediately move to The Villages the next day. But if you do, stay off the road around 4:00 p.m. since golf carts and happy hour do not make for a good combination! More importantly, retirement isn't just about leaving work behind; it's about finding the people, passions, and places that give life meaning.

CHAPTER 12

LIFE ISN'T LINEAR: THE DIVIDENDS OF PERSONAL SETBACKS

interviewed for my first corporate leadership role at the age of twenty-seven. Even at the time, I knew I probably was not ready, but I had been conditioned to believe that success meant constantly reaching for the next rung on the ladder. When I did not get the job, I asked the hiring manager what I could have done differently.

"Be older," he said.

He went on to explain that the interview was largely a courtesy and that he did not place anyone in management under the age of thirty.

I did not yet have a firm grasp on employment law, but I was fairly certain that age was not supposed to be part of the decision. He clarified that it was less about age itself and more about maturity. Leadership, he explained, requires empathy, and people in their twenties often have not accumulated enough life experience to effectively lead teams where nearly everyone is older than they are.

A year later, due to turnover, I found myself back in that same interview room. This time, somewhat reluctantly, I was given the role.

I remained in management for four years before experiencing my first demotion. What felt devastating at the time ultimately proved to be the best thing that ever happened in my career. Ten years as an individual contributor followed. Eventually, I was promoted again into a senior leadership role, only to be demoted a second time. This time, the setback lasted ten weeks rather than a decade. Wholesale changes were no longer required, but meaningful refinements around the edges certainly were.

Along the way, I have both terminated and demoted employees. Anyone who has done both would likely agree that terminating someone is often easier than demoting them. A termination says, "You're on the wrong bus," and while the process is stressful, the relationship typically ends there. A demotion says, "You're on the right bus, just in the wrong seat," and then you continue riding together, often making future interactions more complicated.

The first time I had to demote someone, I found myself thinking back to that original conversation about empathy. I realized I could only truly understand how that individual felt because I had been in that position myself.

It would have been easy to rely on the familiar "right bus, wrong seat" phrase and move on. Instead, we spent time discussing the reality that career progression is rarely linear. We reinforced that the individual was still valued, while also being honest about the skills and development needed to move forward. Recognizing that few people are ready to absorb that conversation in the moment, I always scheduled a follow-up meeting to build a practical game plan.

The lesson is not that you should avoid stretching yourself to prevent disappointment. Slow, steady career progression may be the right path for some, and there is nothing wrong with that. But those willing to take calculated risks may gain something equally valuable, even when the outcome is not what they hoped for: experience, perspective, and empathy they can carry with them for the rest of their careers.

After my first demotion, I decided it was time to get back in shape.

I was overweight, still relatively new in town with a limited social life, and it was clear that both physical health and social connection needed attention if I was going to improve my mental health.

As previously mentioned, I had run cross-country and track in high school. You could say I was good, but not great, and certainly not scholarship material. However, I knew from experience that consistency alone could get me back to a respectable level of fitness. Joining the local YMCA running group that met twice a week for casual three-mile runs was just what the doctor ordered to get me back on the right track. Anyone who runs knows that most training miles should be run at a pace where you can talk but not sing. That guideline led to plenty of conversations during these meetups, some meaningful, but others centered around noncritical topics like favorite Bon Jovi songs.

A small group of us wanted more than six miles per week, so we added a Saturday long run. That's where I met Steve, a fifty-time marathon finisher who volunteered to coach us. At the time, I didn't realize that much of his running advice would later reveal itself as life advice that would heavily influence my still developing leadership style.

Distance running requires discipline anywhere, but training in Florida, especially in the summer, raises the bar. When Steve announced that our long runs would begin at 5:00 a.m., we debated whether he was joking or unhinged. His logic was simple: Finish before the combined temperature and humidity exceeded 150, the point at which dehydration risk outweighs training benefit.

Our long runs increased gradually, with a planned step-back week every few weeks. Steve was firm: Mileage would increase by no more than 10 percent at a time. That meant one additional mile per week until we reached sixteen, then two miles at a time, peaking at twenty-three. Only later did we realize we were training for marathons without ever formally declaring it as a goal.

Florida lacks hills, so we substituted bridges. Early on, I attacked the bridges aggressively, echoing my high school coach's advice to "work the hills." Steve corrected me. In races, he explained, you gain more by pushing on the downhills, where gravity works with you. His other advice was equally simple: Lean into the hill, and don't look up.

Marathon training requires more than long runs. Tempo runs and interval training are essential. To make tempo runs more engaging, we added 5k races to our schedule. As teenagers, we ran those 3.1-mile races at full throttle from start to finish. As adults, that approach produces "positive splits," with each mile slower than the last. The goal Steve taught us was even, or slightly negative, splits.

Race day amplifies effort. The adrenaline of lining up with a thousand other runners can override logic. Before smart watches tracked every metric, you relied on mile clocks and volunteers shouting times. At the first mile marker, you could always identify the newcomers, the ones muttering disbelief at their pace. They had spent everything in the first mile, with two still to go. I was one of them.

Steve avoided the 5k—"I don't like sprints"—but offered advice that stuck. Run the first mile slower than what feels comfortable. Run the second as hard as you can. Then don't let anyone pass you in the third. Twenty-five years later, it remains the best advice I give new runners.

Our long runs eventually became interviews rather than conversations. As marathon day approached, the mental challenge loomed larger than the physical one. We never ran more than twenty-three miles in training, and I worried about the remaining distance. Steve explained that the injury risk of longer runs outweighed the benefit. When you reach mile twenty-three, he said, you have a 5K left, something your body already understands. Visualize your normal weekday route. Then he offered advice that extended far beyond running.

Don't run twenty-six miles. Run one mile, twenty-six times.

Marathon day arrived with one directive: Finish. We did. And on the walk to the post-race celebration, we learned another lesson— walking downstairs hurts more than walking up. The solution? Turn around and walk backward. Your quadriceps will thank you.

Nearly every first-time marathoner declares retirement that same day. Most of them register for their next race the following morning. Too much hard-earned knowledge to waste.

Recovery took a month, but training, and conversation, resumed soon after. One topic kept resurfacing: the lack of specialty running stores in our area. Online retail hadn't yet mastered gait analysis, and runners still needed in-person expertise. We wondered aloud if anyone in our group would be willing to take such a risk and open a boutique shop to serve as our community hub.

One couple that we knew from the running community did just that. Hanging a storefront sign and signing a lease was the easy part. Completing the actual build-out and convincing manufacturers to allow you to carry their product at favorable terms is where things get more complicated.

Four years later, and unbeknownst to the regular customers, they were ready to move on to the next chapter of their lives, focusing on expanding their race management business and family at the same time.

My wife was between careers after years of wholesaling kitchen cabinets through big-box retailers. The 2008 financial crisis had taught her a lasting lesson: When over 80 percent of kitchen remodels are funded by home equity lines of credit, removing those credit lines removes the market. When she returned to work, she wanted passion as much as stability.

Self-employment seemed to offer both, and the decision to open or buy an existing business would benefit from an analytical approach, one involving demographic studies and market data. We chose intuition instead.

We scanned business listings regularly; restaurants, convenience stores, dry cleaners—none resonated. Then we found one titled: "Fitness Enthusiasts Rejoice. A Specialty Retail Opportunity in Seminole County." Five minutes later, we knew it must be our local running store. We were under contract within a week. Ownership transferred in under three months.

The prior owners urged us to attend the annual specialty running retail conference. The organizers granted us early access. In hindsight, it was invaluable.

Trade shows follow a familiar structure: education sessions and an exhibit floor. My wife focused on vendors. I attended the classes. Not all speakers are equal—some are paid to speak; others pay for the audience. Discernment matters.

One insight stood out: Many running stores operated two businesses—retail and race promotion. We chose retail only. Partnering with race directors offered mutual benefit without operational burden.

Specialty retail is destination shopping. Races offered exposure through packet pickup. We placed coupons in race packets, testing $10 off versus 10 percent off. Despite the percentage offering higher savings, the flat $10 coupon was redeemed more than four times as often. People avoid math.

We were also warned about the "friend of the owner" discount. A simple mantra guided us: Give away 10 percent freely; protect 20 percent relentlessly. That made partnerships with schools, charities, and wellness programs easy and sustainable.

Twelve years later, we sold the store to a couple that became instant friends. Whereas the store changed ownership, those life lessons were ours forever, far beyond running and retail.

It took time, and distance, to recognize that none of those moments were isolated. What started as running advice, or retail tactics, or casual observations, eventually revealed a set of recurring principles. They showed up on the road, in business, and later in places I never expected. Looking back, the patterns were remarkably consistent.

One lesson I return to often is the importance of breaking big goals into repeatable units. As Steve said, marathoners don't really run twenty-six miles; they run one mile, twenty-six times. The same pattern shows up in life and in business, where consistency quietly outperforms intensity and clarity routinely beats optimization, much like the humble $10 coupon that proves more powerful than the math suggests. Most important of all: Learn from your mistakes. Failure has a way of disguising its value in the moment, only to reveal later that it was doing the most important training of all.

Back in 1968, Edwin Locke published his pioneering paper "Toward a Theory of Task Motivation and Incentives." He probably had no idea how his focus on micro goals would spark decades of research, as well as an entire industry devoted to goal setting and achievement. An

Amazon search on books on goal setting yields no fewer than 10,000 titles. Make that 10,001 once this book goes to print!

The lesson Steve taught about breaking a marathon into one mile of running, twenty-six times in a row, can be applied everywhere. Whether it's a sports team chasing a championship, or someone simply hoping to lose a few pounds, there are countless ways to succeed. But some methods dramatically increase the likelihood of getting there. Although the cadence of accomplishing multiple micro goals can feel almost ridiculously small, that's exactly why they work.

Dividing large assignments into micro goals can make the most daunting tasks seem more manageable, and setting money aside to prepare for a dignified and fulfilling retirement may be one of the most important ones. Much like career progression, the nonlinear nature of financial markets makes it very difficult to identify at any given time whether progress is being made.

When people read articles about needing $1 million, or $2 million, to retire, it can feel impossible, like staring down a marathon before the first training run. But broken into micro goals, it becomes achievable. For example, a thirty-year-old earning $50,000 a year could reach $1 million by age sixty-five simply by saving 6 percent of their salary into a 401(k) and receiving a 4 percent company match, assuming an 8 percent annualized return (illustrative purposes only—no guarantees). Pay increases and inflation aren't factored in, but if you assume they offset each other, the path to $1 million suddenly feels realistic.

When working with 401(k) participants, we often hear comments like, "It's too late for me," or "I'll probably just have to work forever." While often said half-jokingly, we take those words seriously. Everyone deserves a dignified retirement, and it's never too late to start. Micro goals make the journey possible.

Small, consistent actions have a quiet way of stacking up, even when the scoreboard doesn't immediately reflect it. One mile at a time. One contribution at a time. One disciplined decision layered on top of the last. What feels insignificant in isolation becomes powerful in aggregate.

Life isn't linear, and thankfully, progress doesn't have to be either.

The dividends of personal setbacks often show up later, disguised as resilience, perspective, and staying power. And for those willing to keep moving forward in small, intentional steps, the path has a way of bending back in their favor.

BELTS AND SUSPENDERS: UNNECESSARY RISKS OR MISSED OPPORTUNITIES?

When I was twenty-one years old, I totaled my Subaru sedan while making a left turn onto a four-lane road. The driver in the closest lane kindly gave me the courtesy wave, but I didn't consider that the second lane wasn't planning on yielding. I was banged up after getting hit squarely on the driver's-side door, but fortunately I avoided serious injury.

Our days are filled with risk, many of them so small that our subconscious minds perform quick calculations in microseconds, weighing potential reward against possible harm. Walking across a parking lot in front of a car that sees you is a logical way to reach the store faster, and it's highly unlikely the driver will suddenly step on the gas once you've made eye contact. Still, however small, the risk remains.

Recently, while conducting preliminary due diligence on a potential acquisition for our company, a business broker joked that I'm so risk averse I wear both a belt and suspenders. Of course, that isn't true, but he was trying to make a point, one I saw through, given that he stood to benefit if the deal closed (which it didn't).

The reality is that I'm not opposed to risk. I'm opposed to unnecessary risk, especially when the potential reward doesn't justify it. After my car accident, I realized that most cities are designed so you can make mostly right-hand turns and still get where you're going with minimal delay. How many times have you seen someone speeding through a neighborhood, only to pull up next to them at the same stoplight a minute later?

As a CERTIFIED FINANCIAL PLANNER™, I have a fiduciary duty to put my clients' interests ahead of my own and my firm's. Recommending an investment that doesn't offer the appropriate reward for its risk, and isn't aligned with the client's stated goals, would likely violate the "duty of care" under the CFP® Board's fiduciary standard. And while I'm not obligated to uphold that standard at a cocktail party, I still err on the side of caution in case someone treats the conversation as advice. As a result, I haven't been the most fun guy at parties lately, especially when I questioned the euphoria around Bitcoin.

Whether it's Bitcoin, a "hot stock," or the recent run-up in gold and silver, it's worth asking why you want to own a particular investment. If markets are efficient, as I believe they are, and prices quickly reflect all available information, then the justification can't simply be that you "know it's going higher."

Just like that left turn at twenty-one, most financial mistakes aren't caused by reckless behavior; they're caused by small shortcuts that feel safe in the moment but carry hidden risk. The goal isn't to avoid risk entirely; it's to avoid the kind that doesn't meaningfully improve your odds of reaching your destination. In investing, as in driving, patience and discipline may take a little longer, but they dramatically reduce the chance of getting blindsided along the way.

Contrary to popular belief, the right time for outdoor home maintenance is not when your HOA's compliance committee sends a letter informing you that your curb appeal has lost its, well, appeal. To stay ahead of that necessary but irritating ritual, I power-wash my oak-tree-canopied driveway two or three times a year.

One recent Sunday morning, I rolled out my barely-powerful-enough 1800 PSI Ryobi pressure washer with a twelve-inch surface cleaner. Timing is everything with this task—late enough that I avoid waking the neighbors, but early enough to finish before my friends cruise by with their predictable commentary: "Hey, can you do my driveway next?" or "You know you can pay people to do that!"

That last comment, although intended as a joke, hit harder than expected. My driveway results would earn a grade somewhere between poor and average. How can I spend my workdays explaining the importance of hiring a professional to manage your investments while simultaneously embracing the do-it-yourself mindset at home?

With two hours of mindless manual labor in front of me, I had time to negotiate with myself.

I don't do my own electrical or plumbing work because the risks outweigh the benefits. Beyond the chance of blasting my big toe with a jet of water, there's not much danger in cleaning a driveway.

The same can't be said about financial planning. The risk of doing it incorrectly often outweighs the perceived savings from avoiding advisory fees, or even the pride of making decisions on your own. And while the feedback loop on driveway cleaning is immediate, the feedback loop in investing rarely is.

Fortunately, there's a middle ground. That's the beauty of a fee-only advisory firm. Registered Investment Advisors (RIAs) can charge hourly, per project, or based on assets under management (AUM). AUM remains the most common structure, and for many goal-oriented investors it makes the most sense. But just as I should occasionally hire a professional for a deep clean, DIY investors can continue managing their portfolios while bringing in a CFP® when appropriate for a second opinion.

And for any of my neighbors reading this, my next Sunday project is weeding the flower beds out front. I'll be ready for the drive-by sarcasm I know is coming.

THE LONG VIEW WINS

When my father said those eleven words across the dinner table years ago, I don't think either of us realized how far they would travel. At the time, it was simple, practical advice—file it away and move on. Only later did I begin to understand what was really embedded in that sentence. It wasn't just about income. It was about time. About patience. About the quiet power of decisions that don't look particularly important when you make them.

You've probably noticed it's difficult to neatly classify this work into just one category: leadership, behavioral finance, or even career advice.

That ambiguity is intentional. Lifelong learning doesn't arrive neatly compartmentalized; it shows up in the middle of our daily interactions. As the title suggests, the most valuable lessons are rarely obvious in those seemingly insignificant moments, but instead only after deep reflection, sometimes years or decades later. The moments that shape us rarely look important when they happen, which is exactly why we must learn to recognize and honor them in hindsight.

As a ten-year-old pulling my Radio Flyer classic red wagon down the neighborhood street to collect newspapers, I certainly wasn't thinking about how taking a positive approach to career setbacks would prove valuable later in life. I can say with almost certainty that Michael wasn't excited about the lesson in curiosity he was teaching his new boss while chasing his horse down a country road in Connecticut.

And it's doubtful the young baseball player, while being interviewed at the Little League World Series about discipline, realized his answer was providing guidance to viewers more than twice his age.

I hope you got a few good laughs at my expense along the way. But if that's all you took from these pages, then I haven't done my job. As the subtitle suggests, my hope is that this becomes a practical playbook for you, one that helps you view decisions, habits, and outcomes through a slightly different lens.

Look closely at the small decisions. Own what you do, and take pride in your work, much like the cashier in the big-box home improvement store who refused to let me make a bad purchasing decision. And listen carefully to simple advice that sticks, regardless of the source.

Since you've made it this far, it's fair to acknowledge something you may have already suspected. In my day job, I'm a CERTIFIED FINANCIAL PLANNER™, and the president and cofounder of Strive Retirement Group. Over the years, I've had the privilege of sitting across the table from many thoughtful people making important decisions about their work, their money, and their future.

This book is not meant to be a disguised brochure for that work. In fact, if it reads that way anywhere, I've probably missed what I was trying to do.

The goal here was simpler: to capture the patterns that keep showing up. Treasure the small decisions that matter more than they first appear to, the habits that quietly outperform the flashy alternatives, and the pieces of advice that hold their value longer than expected.

That said, if something in these pages resonated with you and you ever find yourself wanting a second set of eyes on your own decisions, I would genuinely welcome the conversation. No dramatic pitch, just a conversation. You can find me on LinkedIn or through our website—details are included at the end of the book.

And if not, that's perfectly fine too. The ideas should stand on their own.

Much like the marathon runner who retires from the distance only to register for the next race the following morning, this will be my first and last book.

Until the next one… Hope to see you then.

ACKNOWLEDGMENTS

In 1989, needing to find some direction, I was taking a few classes at our local university after realizing that my recently obtained broadcast degree might go unused. While enrolled, I worked as a part-time night shift cashier at Texaco, which had its benefits—free car washes and all-you-can-drink fountain soda. One morning my good friend Rich Gold called me at 11:00 a.m., waking me up to ask for my help. Rich was in his first year as a recruiter for a local employment agency and was told by his manager that he needed to increase his activity. I agreed to go on some interviews, with no intention of taking any of the jobs. However, with wavering commitment, I decided to accept a position with Paychex in Stamford, Connecticut, a firm where I would end up spending the majority of my career. Without that gentle nudge, I may not have had the benefit of learning from some of the brightest mentors, coaches, and leaders in the business.

I want to thank Barbara Leonard for believing in a young, cocky gas station attendant, who showed up at the interview with a brown sports coat and gray slacks. Thank you, Michael McCarthy and Dave Klein, who taught me the difference between leadership and management. And when my career track was anything but linear, thank you for the soft landings, Dan Seyler, Lonny Ostrander, and Michael Majors—I promise you I was paying attention even though it certainly seemed I wasn't.

Thank you, Jim Wright, for your guidance when I pivoted early on to a career in financial services. Fortunately, your advice at the workplace was far more effective than your golf tips. Thank you to my business partners Mark Bentley and Scott Cavanaugh, who took a chance to help launch an advisory firm in its early years, knowing the risks involved.

Thank you to my parents, Edward, and Charlotte Darrow, who allowed me the freedom to make my own choices while still providing the road map along the way. Special thanks to my mother-in-law, Sue McClure, for always treating me like her own son from the first day I met her. Most importantly, thank you to my best friend and wife, April, for going on this amazing, still-in-progress, journey with me over the past twenty-five years!

ABOUT THE AUTHOR

Robert Darrow, CFP®, is a longtime advisor and business professional who has spent his career helping individuals and organizations make better decisions—often by slowing down long enough to understand what experience is trying to teach. He is the president and cofounder of Strive Retirement Group.

Known for his practical perspective and story-driven approach, Robert draws on decades of professional and personal experience to explore how judgment is formed, habits take hold, and outcomes improve over time. His work reflects a belief that wisdom is rarely discovered all at once, but earned gradually through reflection, humility, and attention to everyday moments.

Robert lives in Florida with his wife, April, and their two rescue dogs, Romeo and Juliet. He remains endlessly curious about how small decisions shape much larger results.

STAY IN TOUCH

Website: striveretirement.com
LinkedIn: linkedin.com/in/bobdarrow